# In The Woods, At The Water

## Healing Journeys into Nature

by Jeanne Lightfoot and Bill Ryan

Paintings by Karin Ralph
Book Design by David Lightfoot

Temenos Press
Massachusetts

TEMENOSPRESS

Temenos Press, Box 477, Ashfield, MA 01330
413-625-2828

**Library of Congress Cataloging-in-Publication-Data**

Ryan, William P. and Lightfoot, Jeanne M.

In the woods, at the water: healing journeys into nature/William P. Ryan and Jeanne M. Lightfoot includes bibliographical references.

ISBN 0-9701319-0-9

1. Body, mind and spirit  2. Nature  3. Psychology and psychiatry
4. Self help

First Edition          00 091465          CIP

Printed by Common Wealth Printing Co., Hadley, MA
01035, a Unionized Workers Cooperative. This book is
printed on recycled paper that is 30% post-consumer content.

## DEDICATION

To Bill, with love,
from Jeanne;

To Jeanne, with love,
from Bill;

To our sons,
Mark, Scott, Chris and John

# TABLE OF CONTENTS

# ACKNOWLEDGMENTS

## Jeanne

My deepest gratitude is to Bill. Without his quiet persistence and steadfast determination we would not have completed this book. Thanks to our friend, Royal Brown, whose very early reading of the original proposal gave us a solid direction for the book. I am grateful to my patients for what they have taught me and for allowing me to share their stories. Many thanks to Webster Cotton for working us into his web of friends and connections. Thanks to all our old friends and our new friends for their interest and enthusiasm - Ginny, Ed, Cindy, Bill and Jeannine, Paul, Monica and Bob, Satch and Laura. A special "thank you" to my brother, David, for his creative direction and guidance in designing this book. A great big "Thank You" to family and friends whose financial support made it possible for us to complete this project — my mother, Mary and brother, Joe; Bill's son, Scott and brother, Mike; our friends, Charlotte, Bill and Jeannine. I am grateful to our friend, Karin Ralph, whose lovely paintings have enhanced our work and helped us to create a book that is beautiful. Thanks, always, to my sisters, Mimi and Liz, my dear friend Jean Brown and my mother, Mary, for their constant flow of love and encouragement. I am profoundly grateful to my sons, Chris and John, for their enduring love and, along with Mark and Scott, for their good humor, teasing and tolerance of all our "nature talk." An extra thanks to Chris for all his fine editing work. And again, to Bill, thanks for your unending flow of love, encouragement, and gentle nudging of my creative process.

## ✿ Bill

Several years ago, at the end of a retreat for men that I was co-leading, we were talking about the sense of gratitude all of us felt for what had occurred. I said, sadly, that there were no adequate words in the English language to express the deep, heartfelt sense of gratefulness that we were all feeling. At the end of the gathering one of the men said that there is a West African word that expresses a very large "thank you" – "midassa." To all the following people – *"MIDASSA!!"*

To my beloved mate, Jeanne, with whom it was wonderful to share yet another facet of our adventure. Her personal insights, gift for poetic prose and editorial skills have enriched this work. To my sons, Mark and Scott, whose love and capacity to tease me have sustained us through some difficult years. To my great teachers, the patients who entrust me with their stories. To my mentors, Thoreau and St. Francis, who have walked this path ahead of me. To Chris and John, whose passion for music has reawakened that part of me and who have welcomed this stranger into their lives. To old friends, Ed and Cindy, Bill and Jeannine, Royal and Jean, whose long term support and interest have been sustaining. To new friends Webster, Paul and Jim, who, through the mystery of synchronicity, have entered our lives during this time. To Bob and Monica, Satch and Laura, who have warmly welcomed us into our new home in Ashfield. To Barbara, our agent, who tried unsuccessfully but enthusiastically, to find a publisher for this work. To David, the editor of Pilgrimage, who valued our work and published foreshortened versions of a few chapters. To Karin, whose artistic skill and personal connection to nature have combined to create wonderful paintings. To David, for his expertise in graphic design that helped make this work "beautiful." To Jeanne's mother, Mary; to my son, Scott; to my brother, Mike and Jeanne's brother, Joe; to our friends, Charlotte, Bill and Jeannine — without whose generous financial support this work would not have been published.

## MIDASSA!!!

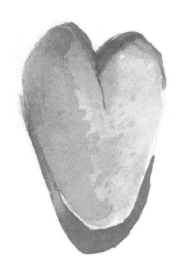

# PREFACE

For over two years, our literary agent tried to find a commercial publisher for this work. Our frequent prayer during that time was that we find the right "home" for our book, a place that would value it and get it out to the right audience. On several occasions we were quite close to negotiating a contract. But, ultimately, we would receive the same response from publishers: they liked the ideas and the writing, but the book wouldn't make any money. Discouraged and disappointed, but not disheartened, we finally decided to self-publish. Once we let go of the idea that the book was going to make money, we felt relieved and excited at the prospect of having total creative control. How freeing! Our prayer, that we would find the right home for our book, was answered, but as is often the case, not in the way we expected.

Immediately, we were flooded with ideas for our new publishing company and about how to design and market the book. Bill chose the name "Temenos" for our publishing company. Temenos is a Greek word meaning a sacred place in nature that is dedicated to a god. Carl Jung also used the term in his analysis of dreams. He thought of Temenos as a sacred, protective enclosure in which we could come to know and nourish the Self. Certainly we think of the nature places described in our book as this kind of sacred place.

Having creative control also meant that we could create exactly the kind of book we wanted. And we wanted this book to be beautiful. We felt that our choice of paper was important and that to include simple ink paintings of these nature places would enhance the beauty of the book and bring the reader into closer connection with what we are saying. We contacted our friend, Karin Ralph, who has translated so beautifully onto paper the images of these places. The paintings are not meant to depict our nature places perfectly, but to evoke for the reader a sense of someplace she or he might have already been, or the desire to seek out a place that is, as yet, unknown.

David Lightfoot, Jeanne's brother, has been our design consultant. His expertise as an artist and graphic designer has helped us with each step along the way: choosing paper and a typeface; deciding on the size of the book and the page design; and laying out the complete manuscript on the computer. His direction was invaluable.

As an example of one of the many synchronistic moments of this long process, we were introduced to a new friend, Paul Bockhorst, by way of his upcoming documentary, "Healing Connections." In many ways, his documentary and our book are mirror image companions. While he was working on his project from the West Coast, we were working on ours from the East Coast.

Just a few closing thoughts about how to use this book. We have written in two voices. Some sections are written by Bill and tell his personal story or stories that involve his work with patients. (Names of patients and some details of their stories have been altered with respect for their privacy.) The sections written by Jeanne indicate the same. Where we use the pronoun "we" or "us", generally, it refers to both Jeanne and Bill unless we are referring to all of us, humankind. Hopefully, this will be easy for the reader to discern. In places where you see this ( ), it indicates either a change in voice from one of us to both of us or a shift in subject matter.

The book has been designed to fit in a backpack or bag and be taken with you as a companion on your nature sojourns. At the end of each chapter are blank pages. These are intended for sketches, musings, poems, journal writing or whatever else your deep Self prompts you to do. We want you, the reader, to experience what we are sharing as little or as much as you want to. Write and draw freely in this book.

Each chapter is an intact essay. The book can be read front-to-back, back-to-front, or you may skip around without losing the message. At the same time, each chapter builds on the one before it.

We hope that making this book has brought more beauty into the world. Please write to us with your reactions. It is in keeping with the tone and the purpose of this book that we would love to hear from you. Please write to us at:

Temenos Press
Box 477
Ashfield, MA 01330


**Enjoy!**

**Jeanne and Bill**

XVI

# INTRODUCTION

It is not just a coincidence that as technology increasingly separates us from nature, we feel more alienated from our inner selves, one another and God. We are suffering from our own lack of connection to nature in ways we are not even aware. While we now know a great deal about the physical consequences of air pollution, clear cutting old growth forests and dumping waste into our waterways, we know very little about the psychological and spiritual losses we suffer from our lack of relationship with nature. We were created to live interdependently with the animals, plants, other creatures and one another. Yet, the current technological world is pulling us from this natural balance into an unnatural state of "relating" primarily to machines. We no longer know or remember that in this interdependent state we can rely on nature to be a healer of our psychological wounds, a source of wisdom in attaining self-knowledge and a catalyst in connecting with God. We hope that the stories and suggestions in this book will help readers to remember this lost knowledge and to recapture this lost connection.

We have come to know nature as a partner in our healing through personal experiences over many years. When we are despairing, fearful, confused or bearing great guilt, we are drawn repeatedly to nature. We return feeling less fearful and guilty and more nourished and able to live in the confusion. As we become more conscious of nature as a living, breathing, active presence in our lives, we want to spend time with her and take care of her as she cares for us. We do not pollute or violate her, not because it is our cause, but because it is unthinkable, just as it is unthinkable to violate our loved ones. When we are in a relationship with another, we give our conscious attention to that person. If we don't, if we spend little quality time together, we become alienated. This process is true with nature just as it is true with the people in our lives.

A number of books currently on the market focus on the healing that comes from time spent alone or on group retreats in the wilderness. Many of these are valuable compilations of writings by poets, environmentalists, ecopsychologists and nature writers. They have played a part in validating and expanding our own notions about our relationship with nature. In truth, no idea is new; we are each tapping into an ancient wisdom that finds expression through our own unique experiences.

As psychotherapists, our focus is on the ongoing relationships in our lives and the need in each of us for healing the wounds that are inevitable on this human journey. While some of what we have read touches on these ideas, what is unique about our work is our emphasis on our relationship with nature and her capacity as healer, as an integral part of our daily lives. We teach our patients how to cultivate this relationship with nature in the midst of day-to-day living. How a walk at the beach, deep into the woods, along the river or time spent in a backyard garden heals us, helps us to know ourselves and connects us to something greater than ourselves. Patients invariably tell us that they feel more centered, less depressed, less alone and significantly quieted down as they begin to be in nature consciously. Nonwestern traditions have always known about nature's healing power and taught that an ongoing relationship is essential for our psychological and spiritual well-being. In an earlier time, Western earth-based traditions also held this wisdom. Patriarchal culture, however, has maintained a position of dominance over nature for so long that we are tragically alienated from her capacity to aid in healing psychological and spiritual wounds.

We don't need to go into the desert for four nights or retreat to the wilderness for an extended period of time to initiate a conscious relationship with nature, although these experiences certainly can be powerfully transformative. In our experience, it is the ongoing relationship with nature as she lives closest to us, returning again and again to a local nature place, that cultivates a sense of deep relatedness and facilitates our healing.

At a time when humankind is on a path toward ecological destruction and faced with increasing alienation, we offer a simple way back to nature and to our natural place in the larger Creation. As we return "home" and rediscover the nourishment and healing available to us from nature, we desire to give back to her in the same way. It is only through a real relationship with nature that we will heal ourselves, our home, Earth, and all of her creatures. Nature is right here, wherever we are. We do not need to seek her somewhere else, but to find her, as it were, in our own backyard.

XXI

## AWAKENINGS

### 🐾 Jeanne

Many years ago, on a visit to see my sisters, I went to Haines Point, a park in Washington D.C. on the edge of the Potomac River. At the far end of this small, city park, I came across an enormous sculpture in the grass of a man, his body half in, half out of the earth. The title of the sculpture, by J. Seward Johnson Jr., was "The Awakening." I was powerfully struck by this image and stood contemplating it for a long while. The sculpture gave form to something that was stirring within me. All these years later this is the image that comes to mind as I think about what it means to "awaken." As the memory floats around in my mind, all kinds of phrases wander through to try and describe it: it is as if the man is being birthed from Mother Earth; he is emerging from the darkness; he is coming back from the dead; he is waking from a dormant state. I can use any of these to describe the image, it doesn't matter. Each one attempts to put words to the experience of "awakening."

For me, the metaphor of awakening is the perfect way to describe what it feels like to become "Self-conscious," to become aware of our deep Self or higher Self. It is as if we are asleep and then suddenly we wake up. Our consciousness expands and we see ourselves and our world in a different way. Previously held beliefs about who we are and where we fit in the world fall away. It is as if a veil has been removed from our eyes and what was obscured is now seen clearly.

While an awakening experience can feel sudden, it usually does not happen without preparation, and is often brought on by overwhelming pain, a crisis or a loss of some kind. In the sculpture, the man has an agonized look on his face. It is not easy for any of us to let go of what we have always believed to be true about ourselves and to look at the deeper truth of who we are. In fact, this is the most difficult task of all. It is also the most important if we are to express our true complexity and authenticity through our creativity, our interdependence, our darkness and our capacity for compassion and love – if we are to be fully human.

Before we are awakened, the deep Self is often nearly dead, dormant, buried or suppressed. In a lifetime, we wake many times to this Self and, while pain is frequently a catalyst, we can also be awakened to our true nature through relationship or experiences of great beauty and profound joy. In the East, these awakenings might be called "samadhis" or small enlightenments. "Show me your original face before you were born," the Zen Master might say to his student. What is our true nature before we are socialized by family, church, school and culture? To awaken to this is our greatest privilege and our deepest, though often hidden, desire.

❦

For Bill and I, nature has been a constant companion through our many experiences of awakening. We were not always aware of her presence, but only know it in retrospect.

2

But, as we have become conscious of nature's role in our journeys, her companionship has enhanced our experiences and she has become a significant catalyst in continuing to know our deep Self. Nature wakes us from the illusion that we are separate from each other and from her. She awakens us to our "creature" nature and to feelings of connection to something greater than ourselves. Through what John Fowles calls the "creative ferment"[1] she stirs the creativity deep within each of us. Nature wakes us to beauty, bounty and aliveness. She awakens us from the deep sleep of not seeing. She awakens us to the presence of our own soul, our true nature and the soul of all creation.

If we think back, most of us had a connection to nature in childhood, however slight it may have been. Just as pondering our history with the significant people in our lives can strengthen and enhance our human relationships, remembering our earlier bond with nature can help us to reconnect with her as adults. We all have nature stories. Some of us grew up near the sea, or on a farm or by a lake surrounded by woods. Being in nature has been such an integral part of our lives from the beginning that we cannot imagine a period of separation. Some of us had early transcendent experiences that formed a bond with nature that has never been broken. Most of us, however, lost this childhood connection to nature somewhere along the way. Because we spend so much time indoors, or with computers, cars and other machines, we have become estranged from our Mother. And, even when we do have experiences in nature, we are not conscious of their meaning or impact on our lives. In his essay, "Nature," Ralph Waldo Emerson wrote:

> To speak truly, few adult persons can see nature. Most persons do not see the sun.

At least they have a very superficial seeing. The sun illuminates the eye of the man, but shines into the eye and the heart of the child. The lover of nature is he whose inward and outward senses are still truly adjusted to each other, who has retained the spirit of infancy even into the era of manhood. His intercourse with heaven and earth, becomes part of his daily food. In the presence of nature, a wild delight runs through the man, in spite of real sorrows.[2]

In other words, it is the child self that is connected to nature. Nature awakens the child self who, in turn, wakes the adult self. When we are young, consciousness of our relationship with nature is not so important. As we lose that childhood purity of experience, however, our alienation from nature increases. If we are to awaken to nature and allow her to be a catalyst to awakening to our deep Self, then we must open our eyes and ourselves to the impact of nature in our lives.

***

## Bill

Until I was nine, I lived in a city apartment. My only contacts with "nature" were on family outings to the local park, visits to the zoo or a trip to the Coney Island seashore. None of these left much of an impression on me. When I was nine, my family moved to a housing project in Staten Island that was bordered on one side by woods. This is where my relationship with nature began. Both of my parents worked long hours so I spent a good deal of time roaming these woods eating wild blackberries, playing Robin Hood with bows and arrows and exploring local "Indian caves" searching for arrowheads. These woods were a place of refuge for me from the problems caused by my father's alcoholism and the daily humiliations of a childhood spent in the psychological war zone of a housing project. Though I did not think about it at the time, nature was healing for me. I would go to the woods to lick my wounds and heal my heartache. This was the beginning of a lifelong experience of nature as a sanctuary.

In my mid-twenties, the woman I loved left me for someone else. Devastated and humiliated by the loss, I spent a period of time trying to numb the pain by drinking and involving myself with one woman after another. When this failed, I went on a 15,000-mile, three-month, solo journey around the country and into Canada. I spent that time almost entirely outside, hiking to the bottom of the Grand Canyon; walking for hours along the magnificent beaches of California and Oregon by day and sleeping on their sands at night; swimming in rivers, lakes and oceans; hiking up mountains; trekking in desert sands. Much of the time, my lost love was on my mind. One night, while I was sitting at a picnic table in a wooded roadside rest area, I began sobbing and praying desperately, "Please help me." I was raised a Catholic and had even studied for a while to be a priest, but I had left that behind and did not consider myself to be religious or spiritual. I rarely, if ever, prayed and had little connection to God. My prayer came from my woundedness and despair. I did not know how I could endure feeling so empty and alone. After a while, something shifted in me. I felt quieted down and no longer alone. I felt that my prayer had been answered in a deeply personal and inexplicable way. Looking back, this was my first personal experience of God's presence. In my state of unconsciousness and deep sleep at the time, I did not really understand or have words to articulate what had occurred. But now I understand this transcendent experience as a moment of communion between my soul and God. I know, too, that nature had been the catalyst. The prolonged period of time in nature coupled with my emotional neediness had created a receptive space for something to enter. Today, I call that grace. It was one of those moments in a lifetime that is mysterious and sacred, that we understand in different ways as we age and, hopefully, grow in wisdom.

In my adult years, I have always enjoyed spending time in nature, whether snorkeling in Mexico, walking in local woods or meditating in some quiet spot outside. I have a long-standing relationship with trees — we share the common trait of height — and often call myself a "walking around tree." My time outside has grown more precious and valued over the years, yet only recently have I awakened to the beckoning of nature as a place of healing and connection to my higher Self and God.

A few years ago, I initiated the ending of a 24-year marriage. The painful loss of connection to my wife, children, friends, home and community was wrenching. The guilt of causing them so much pain overwhelmed me. It almost broke me. I would have welcomed death, and several times I thought of crashing my car. Anything to rid myself of the pain and guilt I felt. For the first six months of this time, I lived alone in a dormitory on the campus of a small college that was no longer operating. I shared the surrounding acres of woods, fields, ponds and stretch of beach with two grounds keepers, their families and an occasional visitor.

Each of the many magical nature spots there became a refuge from my overwhelming guilt and a source of deep healing. I spent hours every week walking the grounds, sitting in meditation on a tree stump in the woods, surrendering myself to the healing power of nature. She is the one who carried me through my pain to a place of eventual peace. After a while, I moved to a place that is surrounded by 800 acres of wooded park land. A short walk from my home, these woods became my new sanctuary. When I left the road and entered the pine grove, I moved from the mundane world into a sacred place. All those long years ago, as a young man traveling across the country, I had come to nature for healing. At that time, the experience was unconscious. It is only in retrospect that I realize the healing aspects of that journey. This time, in my wooded sanctuary, the healing became conscious and thus more powerful. Nature awakened me to her bountiful capacity to heal my wounded heart and comfort my sorrowing soul. Early on I was drawn to a spot where two ancient pine trees stand. I thought of these trees as my "Mother" and "Father" trees. After a time, they came to symbolize the male and female aspects of God. Oftentimes, I would fall to my knees by my trees and, sobbing, ask for forgiveness. Here I was not judged or burdened with additional guilt. I did enough of that to myself. Emerson recognized this healing quality of nature when he wrote about the time he spent in the woods during periods of struggle.

"There I feel nothing can befall me in life – no disgrace, no calamity (leaving me my eyes), which nature cannot repair."[3] In among the trees, I felt comforted and nourished. I would hug the trees, touch their leaves and branches. Here I had a consoling mother and a father who modeled the strength I needed to continue my journey. I had died, not in the literal sense, of course, but psychologically. Nature took me through the painful rebirthing process, awakening me to a new and more complex Self.

Today my relationship with nature is a conscious one. She has awakened me to her awesome powers, her sensual beauty, and to my own deep Self. Now, when I am struggling, disconnected from myself or just weary, I know she is waiting for me. Nature is a source of consolation, guidance, companionship, refuge and recharging. I seek her out. She is always there and never judges how I am feeling, what I have done or who I am. Our relationship is one of mutuality and communion. I want to do things for her, take care of my nature place, in gratitude for her loving care and attention. I love her.

### 🌹 Jeanne

As Bill's story relates, nature is a healing place whether we are conscious of that or not. Yet, that power is greatly increased when we become aware of her capacity for healing. Perhaps that knowledge is inherent in children and that is why we so often went outdoors to get away from difficulties at home. As a girl, I was outside as much as possible. In part, perhaps, to escape the dark, dank feeling of depression that hung so heavily in my home. I would be climbing trees, making a secret hideout in the "sticker bushes," building a tree-house in the apple tree in our backyard, or swinging on the swing just to feel the cool air caress my face and watch the blue sky glide back and forth before my eyes. I can remember one summer evening hanging upside down on the monkey bars in a neighbor's yard and watching the sunset. So engrossed was I in the magical colors of the sky, that I fell on my head! But I loved the sunsets and would always stop what I was doing to watch for awhile. My mother gave me that gift. I remember warm evenings when she would stop in the middle of preparing dinner for our large family and stand out on the front porch and watch the sun go down. I loved to watch with her. "Oh, look at this beautiful sky!" she would cry out with a passion I seldom saw in her. She felt the sunset. She was touched by the pink-green-orange-purple beauty of the sky. I stood alongside her with a sense of awe for the scene unfolding before us.

"Nature," in the potato fields-turned-suburbia where I grew up, was quite tame. I wonder how much deeper my connection to her would have been had I lived my early years in a "wilder" place. For now, when I am in the country, walking through the woods or climbing along the rocks of a stream, I am touched in this deep part of my Self that says, "This is where I should have grown up. This is where I should've been a girl." As a young wife and mother I often went camping with my family, but by that time my capacity for really experiencing nature had been dormant for some time. Not until I went into therapy, divorced my husband, quit my job as a bookkeeper and came to work at a small college near my home did my relationship to nature and my Self change forever. I return to that place now to remember my awakening.

❦

Recently divorced, I first came to the campus of this small, private college situated on an old estate in the mid 1980s for a job interview. Instantly, I was captivated. This place was idyllic. Lush, green lawns rolled gracefully down to the sandy shore of the Long Island Sound, edged on either side in an array of vibrant, autumn trees. I could feel the hunger inside of me to be surrounded by such beauty. I wanted that job badly! With the Sound on one side, turtle-filled ponds on another, a small woods, open fields, and a host of unusual people, this place beckoned every part of me. While the pay was low and the job itself quite ordinary, it offered me opportunities I would not have had otherwise. But the place, the land, drew me most. I felt so blessed to work every day in what was essentially a nature sanctuary. It was here, in this "sacred place," that I began my conscious relationship with nature. For the next six years, I was awakened by nature to her beauty, initiated into her mysteries and comforted by her ever-presence.

As I sit here now, looking out over the barely-rippling water, feeling the gentle touch of the breeze on my skin, listening to the chatter of the birds and the hum of the locusts, I slip easily into a state of remembering. In those days my greatest pleasure was to leave the office and go for a solitary walk at lunchtime, on a break or sometimes in the evening when I'd stay late for a student function. I wandered the rocky, narrow strip of beach barefoot, lost in thought about some current struggle, pining an unrequited love or simply taking in the intense beauty and wonder of this place. I collected hundreds of stones and pieces of broken shells from the beach. Each one was chosen for a particular reason, the color reflecting my mood in that moment , the shape or texture evoking a deep feeling that I could not articulate. Often, I would burst into tears on my daily sojourns, not always understanding why. I struggled with so much in those years. I wanted to be a good mother to my sons, to be present with them emotionally. I was trying to keep things going on very little money. I enrolled in college. And, I was getting to know my Self in so many different ways. My life was wide open, exciting, a whole new adventure. And, I was exhausted. I am grateful to this place, profoundly grateful to nature for guiding me and nurturing me through those difficult and tiring times. Of course, she was not my only guide, but a powerful one indeed. Nature drew me deep into my unconscious and led me into the moist, dark, rich corners of my psyche.

Oh, this is a sacred place. I can feel it all around me, smelling the sweet scents wafting on the breeze that caresses me so very gently. Sometimes I feel intoxicated with the smells, just as the damp, musky smells of my lover intoxicate me. During my years here I learned that this land was originally in the care of Native Americans. One of the grounds keepers has a collection of arrowheads and pottery shards that he has gathered over time. In my mind's eye, I imagine sacred fire ceremonies on this land, offerings to the Great Mother, women gathering together in the far field during their moon time, away from the men, tending and nurturing each other and renewing their creative spirit through the power of the new moon.

I rarely understood what was happening to me in those years. I had been trying to live for so long from my rational mind, now I was immersed in emotion, texture, feeling, color, form. Nature seemed to be a mirror of my inner landscape. As my connection to her deepened, I felt the pull of her energy, her urging me to move more deeply into my Self, and I responded. I knew that what was happening in me was powerful, but I didn't have the language to describe it. Poetry became a way for me to communicate with my deep Self. It is, after all, one of the languages the soul speaks. Nature, it seemed, was inside as well as outside of me:

> A tree is erupting within me
> I am filled with waterfalls and
> mountains and raging rivers.
> Shall I walk among the mountains,
> cross the raging rivers,
> climb my tree?
> And when I'm through immerse
> myself under my very own
> waterfall!

One day, I saw the earth beneath me breathe. I was anguished, hurting, in intolerable pain. As I walked from place to place, looking for consolation in the woods or along the shore, I was unable to stop sobbing. It was winter, the ground was partly frozen and everything around me was intensely beautiful. I had never noticed the beauty of winter before coming to this place: the intense magenta branches on unmasked bushes; the soft, golden-yellow-orange sea grass; the rich, earthy-brown tree bark that became richer still in the winter rain; the vast array of winter greens. Had I never before seen the bright red-yellow of the bittersweet vine? This day the colors were so vibrant, so alive. I, too, was alive and writhing in my pain. I could find no place of comfort. And then I saw the ground before me rise and fall, rise and fall with each breath of the Great Mother. I would have thrown myself on this gently heaving breast of my Mother and nestled my tear-stained face in the warmth of her bosom, but I felt self-conscious and somewhat frightened. I did not fully understand the power of the life energy beneath me or my own connection to that life. At the same time, I was consoled.

I wrote a song in this deep, rich, earthy, moist, watery Mother place. After awhile, I began to understand this "awakening" process. My song was in gratitude and reverence to nature and the mothering I received from her at a time when I so desperately needed it:

Rest this child in your arms
Momma, she is weary
so much to reap
yet still so much to sow
lay down her head
with grasses all around her
the comfort of your breast
will bring her peace.

Your waters soothe
and are a consolation
the trees reach out to comfort
with their limbs
the wind blows soft and low
as it caresses:
your rest will come
don't fear, your rest will come.

I still come to this mothering place. In the summertime, Bill and I spend long Sundays resting and restoring ourselves from the work week and from all the time spent taking care of others. We walk, meditate, read, sleep, talk, swim, whatever it is we need at that moment. At other times, we each come here alone as I have today. She still beckons me with her sweet smells carried by the wind, with the sound of her voice rustling through the trees, with the silent, unspoken urging that draws me to her. She calls out to me, "Come, spend a little time here with me so that you can remember who you are. You are a child of nature, not separate from or outside of, but a creature just like the others, of my forests, fields, water. You are my daughter. Remember you are my daughter and do not be afraid. I am here always. I am your original Mother."

I know that this place will not always be here for me, not as it has been or is now. The campus is closed, it is only a matter of time before some other owner comes along and I will no longer be free to come and go as I am now. When that time comes, I will move on. I will listen again for her beckoning. I will find another mothering place and nestle myself contentedly there in her bosom for a time. And, I will be then as I am now, eternally grateful for her presence.

***

## 🌸 Bill

Caitlin, a dancer and choreographer in her mid-thirties, was very connected to nature as a child. She remembers herself as a "secret nature girl." Caitlin had always been deeply intuitive, but as a child was made to feel horrible about the "sensitive" parts of herself. Her artistic, creative, emotional self was criticized and condemned. Thus, emerged her need for a "secret" relationship with nature. While Caitlin's parents were physically present, they were not available emotionally. Her mother suffered with depression for many years and her father was a "big bear" who would rear up in angry, bellowing rages of frustration. Caitlin recalls, at the age of three, running from the house and sitting under a tree sobbing. She knew, in the way of a three-year old, that her mother and father were unavailable to her. Her cat came along then, purring and rubbing up against her and nestled himself into her lap. She was consoled. Looking back, Caitlin feels this was the beginning of her relationship with nature. At times, she felt like a feral child. The cats, not her parents, had raised her. They provided her with a consistent source of unconditional love.

During her late teens and twenties, Caitlin danced with the Rockettes, off-Broadway shows and national tours of Broadway musicals. She flourished as a dancer but her relationship with nature grew dormant, as it does with so many of us. It was only as she struggled in therapy with issues of low self-esteem and difficulty in knowing her true Self, that the story of her early connection to nature began to emerge. When Caitlin initially talked with me about her early experiences in nature, she spoke in a whisper as if revealing a secret. This is not unusual. Oftentimes, in individual sessions and in workshops, people relate the story of their history with nature as if they are discussing a secret life openly for the first time. As in Caitlin's case, this often results from childhood experiences of constant criticism. But our culture also engages in a denigration of anything that appears "odd." A child who makes friends with the creatures of the woods is likely to be teased and tormented verbally, called "strange" or "weird."

And, while it is true that certain children develop a strong bond with nature because nurturing human relationships are lacking, the ability to compensate in this way is not crazy but a blessing. Many adults feel that nature saved them from the chaos of their childhood.

Cautiously, lest I think of her as crazy, over time Caitlin continued to tell me her story. As a teenager she always loved walking in the woods and talking with her "elder" trees, particularly her "Grandfather tree." Even when she was traveling and dancing and her time in nature was infrequent, she would find herself drawn back to this place during periods of great pain. With the ending of a relationship, the loss of a dance partner to AIDS, or periods of uncertainty and confusion, Caitlin would return to her Grandfather tree. Sitting beneath the tree sobbing, mourning the loss of a lover or a friend, she felt consoled, just as she had as a child. In her work with me, by strengthening and affirming her impulse to go into nature when she is troubled, Caitlin has become aware that this is a relationship she has with nature. She comes to her Grandfather tree vulnerable, open and trusting and leaves feeling comforted, grateful and less burdened. Caitlin now consciously seeks out nature places. With her renewed awareness of the importance of this relationship, her "nature girl" self has been reawakened. Only this time she is not secretive about it. Her work with me has powerfully affirmed that essential aspect of her deep Self.

As she so often does, nature continues to urge Caitlin to fully reclaim her Self. She has always had difficulty accepting herself as a powerfully intuitive, creative and sensitive woman. These are the parts of Self that were condemned in childhood and so went into hiding. While attending Jeanne's workshop for women on awakening intuition, Caitlin had another powerful nature experience that further affirmed the emergence of her true Self. Off on a solitary walk, she returned to a spot she had found at an earlier workshop of ours. This time she was drawn to a particular tree in the same area. Each time she tried to go forward on her walk, she was drawn back to the tree. Finally, a thick, gnarled, viney staff just her height caught her eye. It was leaning against the tree. Caitlin reached for it and stood with it at her side. As she did, a vivid image came into her mind: she stood in an ancient forest, staff in hand, feet slightly apart, her thick, wavy, red hair hanging full and free over her shoulders. She was startled by her garb – the full warrior gear of a Viking! For several minutes Caitlin remained silently focused on this image in her mind's eye. As she did, she felt in her body her strength, energy and power as a woman. She stood erect and strong, fully connected to her warrior self.

Carrying her wooden staff, Caitlin returned late to the workshop. Time had stood still, she had no awareness she had been gone so long. As she shared her story with the other women, tears streamed down her face. She had given up so much of herself for so long, she told them, her strength, her sensitivity, her creativity. Grasping her staff, the symbol now of her feminine power, she told the other women with conviction, "I will not give up parts of my Self for others anymore!"

To know ourselves deeply, to know, as the Buddhists say, our "true nature," is our greatest privilege and our deepest desire. Nature can help to wake us from the slumber that keeps us trapped behind the mask of the false Self. Listen to her beckoning and go into the woods, down by the river, to the edge of the ocean, into a field of tall grass and wild flowers, up to the mountain top. Let nature reveal herself to you and in so doing awaken you to your deeper Self, to your full potential, to the truth of who you really are.

# PRESENCE

Nature is a great teacher. We can learn many things from her. But if we are not present to her, we will miss what she has to offer us. We are drawn to nature, sensing, perhaps, the possibilities there. But then we run past it, bike through it, or walk in it with headphones on. Because of our own distractions, we are not truly present and we miss her teachings. To be present means, simply, to pay attention. And, yet, presence is the most difficult thing of all. It is required of us all the time: as mates, parents, friends, at work, in school, in church, reading a book, listening to music. Each of these requires our presence and yet we have what the Buddhists call "monkey minds," minds that constantly jump from one place to another like monkeys in trees. We are always thinking about something other than what is happening now. We are thinking about the argument we had with our mate two days ago, or the one with our father ten years ago, or about the presentation we have to give at work next week, or about what we want for dinner tonight. How difficult it is to remain present to what is happening from moment to moment! And, yet, when we do, life is richer, deeper and more spontaneous.

The way to be present in nature is through our senses. Nature beckons us constantly through our senses, extending her hand to us "in friendship" and inviting us to "share her beauty"[4] as Kahlil Gibran so aptly describes. But our senses have been dulled over time either from the overstimulation of too many images and too much noise, or from a general shutting down of self. So often as children we were told how we should or should not feel that we began early on to close ourselves down to what we were truly feeling. Because we experience our feelings through our bodies and our bodies experience through our senses, when our feelings shut down our senses are dulled. If we are to be present in nature, open and receptive from moment to moment, then we must reawaken our senses.

Through smelling, touching, listening, tasting and looking nature beckons, "Come into me, partake of my beauty and my bounty. Be present here with me." Oftentimes, on the way to our favorite nature sanctuary, we drive down a certain road lined on either side with huge, old trees. The trees reach out their limbs and greet us as we go by, welcoming us. In the woods, the birds sing all around us, inviting us to listen. The leaves of the trees and bushes, blown gently by the wind, wave as we walk by. We return their greeting with a touch. The scent of honeysuckle wafts beneath our noses and we accept the invitation to partake of this delightful taste treat. The sensation of the wind on our skin stirs us. It wakes us to what is invisible and mysterious. The roar and flashing of a thunder and lighting storm reminds us of nature's awesome and sometimes awful power. In the woods two paths converge and we are beckoned by "the one less traveled" into her mystery, into the unknown. A rocky stream bed invites us to climb. A grassy meadow offers a place of respite for a while. To be present we must be open to this beckoning. Our senses must be receptive.

One way to learn presence is through meditation. The practice of meditation has been a central part of all the great religious and spiritual traditions as a way of coming closer to God. Early Jewish mystics had a tradition of daily outdoor meditation. The author of *The Cloud of Unknowing* speaks almost ecstatically of the contemplative life.[5] Buddha was the master of meditation, continuing for nine years under the Bodhi tree until he reached enlightenment. With the recent surge of interest in Eastern spiritual traditions, the long-forgotten practice of meditation has gained popularity. Meditation quiets the mind, stills the body and teaches us to be mindful, to observe ourselves in each moment. Having practiced mindfulness meditation for the past fifteen years, we can attest that this is very helpful. Raised in a culture of distractions, meditation is a useful and powerful tool. We can bring the practice of mindfulness meditation into nature to help us be more present there. Mindfulness, quite simply explained, is a process of watching thoughts and other distractions as they come and go and focusing our attention on our breathing. When we pay attention to our breath and do not get attached to the distractions that constantly come along, our bodies relax and we become more open and receptive. The effects of meditation, however, are subtle and slow, realized over a long period of time and often noticed only in retrospect. Do not expect much at first, but make the practice of mindfulness a part of daily life. Bring a meditative quality to your time in nature, even for a few moments, and you will begin to feel the benefits after awhile. You will realize that you are more present to your Self, your mate, your children, your work. And, when your attention wanders, you will be able to bring it back to the present moment.

To learn to be mindful and present in nature, go alone into your favorite place there – the woods, a meadow, down along the water's edge, up among the hills or mountains. It is important to go alone, especially at first. If someone is with you, he or she will become a distraction. (We will explore going into nature with others in a later chapter.) For now make this a solitary journey. As you enter this special place, consciously tell yourself that you are leaving the ordinary world and entering a sacred space. This is important since presence has nothing to do with time and space as we normally experience them but everything to do with a state of consciousness. Moving into nature, you are leaving the ordinary consciousness of day-to-day living. As you enter this sacred place, begin to pay attention to your breathing. Initially, allow yourself to take several deep breaths. Breathe in through your nose and out deeply through your mouth. As you breathe out imagine letting go of all thoughts, concerns and worries of the outside world. While this may seem a simple thing to do, in actuality, it is not. Our monkey mind always gets in the way. This is, however, the beginning of presence. Thoreau, the well known 19th-Century nature mystic, spent several hours each day walking in nature. In his essay "Walking", he laments how often he would find himself still with "thoughts of the town" even though he had already walked a mile into the country.[6] Most of all, be gentle with yourself and non-judgmental. Thoreau was an expert and yet had to continually "practice" presence. You may need to come back to these deep, letting go breaths often, especially as you begin this practice.

After several of these releasing breaths, allow your breathing to return to its natural rhythm, still focusing your attention on each breath as you inhale and exhale. Thoughts will continue to come into your mind. Notice them, let them go and allow your attention to return once again to your breathing. Thoughts in the mind are like those big, fluffy clouds against the blue sky: they float along in the sky, changing shape constantly, but the vast blue sky in the background remains constant. It is into this "big mind" of the open blue sky that we want to move. Here we are less distracted, more open and receptive. After several minutes of following each breath, begin to notice nature's presence. Notice first the feel of the breeze or wind on your skin. If it is fall or winter and you are wrapped up tight in warm clothing, feel the coldness of the air on your face. Close your eyes and really feel it. If it is spring or summer, feel the breeze wherever it touches your skin. Close your eyes and really feel it. Spend several minutes focusing on this sensation, taking it in fully with each breath. Be fully present to the wind. You are in the wind, the wind is in you. Do the same with the sensations of the sun, rain, snow or whatever else is touching your skin. Reach out and feel the bark of a tree, touch the leaves or rocks, feel the grass or sand beneath your feet. Take in each experience of this surrounding presence on your breath, letting thoughts come and go. If you need to, take some deep, letting go breaths, exhaling deeply and releasing whatever may be keeping your mind distracted. Do not rush, spend some time with the sensation of touch. Stay with this meditation until you are fully aware of the presence of nature touching your skin.

Now let your attention move gently to your sense of smell. This sense is a very powerful but underdeveloped one in most of us. Do not be surprised if it takes several trips into nature to begin to notice smells. We have learned from the animals that if you tilt your head back slightly and take in short, rapid sniffs you can begin to smell the very subtle scents that might go unnoticed. This is because the olfactory receptors are way at the back of the nose. Sniffing in this way gets the smells back there. Or, you can take deep, gentle breaths in through your nose and carry them all the way down into your belly. Sometimes we use the rapid sniffs to catch something wafting by on a breeze and then, when we have it, close our eyes and breathe it in deeply. If you need to, go back and focus on the breath, deep, releasing breaths if needed, and then return to the smells around you. Once accustomed to experiencing the presence of smells you may find them intoxicating and arousing. Natural smells are very erotic and sensual. We are so heavily perfumed and deodorized, however, that we have forgotten this. Again, take your time. Allow yourself to become fully aware of the smells of nature as they come into your body on your breath. Close your eyes and breathe in the smells.

Now slowly allow your focus to move to the sounds around you. Take a few breaths and then listen. "I had no idea nature made so much noise," wrote Richard Powers.[7] When you begin to listen in a conscious way, you will find out how often this is true! What do you hear? Are there birds twittering, wind rustling through the leaves of the trees, sounds of crashing waves, water rushing over rocks, creaking tree branches weighed down with snow or ice? Listen. Take the sound in, not only through your ears, but also on your breath. Breathe in the sounds. Again, if thoughts come into your mind, let them come and go and bring your attention back to your breath. Listen again. Close your eyes and listen. Take the time and feel the full presence of sounds as they enter you. Feel yourself fully present to listening.

Return to your breath for a moment or two and now, if possible, engage your sense of taste. Pick ripe and juicy raspberries or blueberries. If you're at the beach, put your hand in the salt water and then put your fingers in your mouth. Take a piece of tall grass and chew on it for a while. Put a stone in your mouth and suck on it. Follow the scent of the honeysuckle, pluck a flower, bite off the end and sucking in, relish that one delightful moment of sweetness. How do these things taste in your mouth? Use your breathing to take them in fully. Close your eyes and slowly, with awareness, take in the fullness of taste and sensation.

Focusing on your breath once again, move to the sense of sight. As you have noticed with each of the other senses, we closed our eyes for a part of the time. This is because our sense of sight is overdeveloped. It tends to overpower the other, less developed, senses. Just as a blind person's other senses develop more acutely to compensate for the loss of sight, we can begin to develop our senses of smell, touch, taste and hearing if we can block out sight. But, we are visual creatures also and so we must not neglect this sense. In fact, this practice of presence is really a way of "seeing" differently. We are practicing a different kind of awareness. And, by opening to a greater awareness of and presence to our other senses, you may find that when you look around now, you are actually seeing differently. But first, pay attention to your breathing for a moment. All of your senses are heightened. You are hearing, feeling, smelling and tasting with greater intensity. All of your senses are open and receptive. Now, slowly begin to look around. Bring the same attention, the same presence, to seeing that you have brought to your other senses. Look at the sky, the water, the grass, the trunks of trees, the rocks. Are the colors more vibrant, the textures more defined? Are you seeing more intensely and intently than before? Again, take in the experience on your breath. Use your breath to remain fully present to each of your senses, taking in the smells, sounds, textures, tastes and sights around you. Be fully present in nature and allow nature to be fully present in you.

***

By opening our senses and becoming more receptive to nature, we can begin to take in her teachings. First, nature teaches us to be our true Self. This is so simple and yet so profound. Look around again. Do you ever see a tree trying to be a rock? Or a rabbit trying to be a bird? Does a willow try to be an oak? Or a cricket try to "caw" like a crow? You will never see any of this in nature. And yet we humans spend half of our lives, sometimes our whole lives, trying to be someone or something or some way that is out of harmony with our basic nature. In nature a tree is just a tree. A rabbit is only a rabbit. A willow does not try to be an oak. How simple, how profound! When we allow ourselves to be fully present in nature our deepest Self, our true nature, longs to respond to this Mother's urging to be ourselves. We are deeply touched by this beckoning to go within, to stop trying to be who we are not, to discover who we really are. Responding to this invitation, however, means not judging ourselves. This is nature's other great teaching.

Because we have been judged and criticized as children, we have internalized voices that repeat these early judgments and criticisms over and over to our adult selves. We then project these critical voices onto other people in our lives and we are sure they are judging us also. We can hardly come clear of this inner self-criticism and these outer projections long enough to be our real selves. But, nature never judges us. She envelops us with her beauty and the bountiful affirmation to be who we really are. When we are in nature our projections diminish. It is hard to project a critical voice onto a tree. It is difficult to imagine the ocean or a river judging us. So these voices and projections are quieted down considerably. We are freer to explore our true depth and nature as a unique human being in the nonjudgmental presence of Mother Nature.

But, how do we do this? How do we explore our true Self in nature? First, we must respond to her beckoning; answer her invitation and see where it leads. Follow what feels right. Recently, we went four-wheeling along a beach with some friends. Stopping in a spot with some high bluffs, we climbed to the top for a better view. After a while we began walking down but Bill stopped midway. While we waited for him at the bottom, he suddenly took off his shoes and socks, threw them to us along with his glasses, laid on the ground and rolled down the remainder of the bluff. We all had a good laugh when he got to the bottom! He looked like a ten-year old in a 6'6" body! Being on that sand dune provided an opportunity for the suppressed, playful self to emerge without criticism and judgment. Bill needed only to respond to the urge from inside and the invitation from the outside.

What is this "urge" from inside that we need to respond to? It is our "sixth sense," intuition. A host of external sources in the family, church, school and the wider social and political culture are continually telling us what to do, what is good for us. As a result, our inner sense of what is really best for us is usually quite underdeveloped. In some of us, the intuitive sense of what we need to do from moment-to-moment is dormant. In others, it is nearly dead. When we are in nature and our senses are heightened and our projections and self-criticism diminished, our intuition can be reawakened. Without distractions, the inner urge is heard more clearly. As we walk along following our breath, a certain thought, impulse or image may enter our mind unexpectedly. It may be an urge to walk down a side trail rather than the path we planned to take. It may be an impulse to climb onto a rock, plunge into the water, sit on a fallen log or make an angel in a field of pristine snow. It may be an image of lying in a grassy field, or a line from a song that repeats over and over in our mind and wants to be sung out loud. It may be an impulse to gather stones along the beach. Who knows where the urge comes from, but in a magical and mysterious way some aspect of our inner being is responding to nature at that moment in a way that is uniquely ours. It is a moment of communion, play or sharing. It is a moment of relationship.

## 🐚 Jeanne

A couple of months ago, I went out to my writing spot beneath some trees overlooking the water. I had every intention of writing, but each attempt was futile. I was yawning and felt quite sleepy, though it was only late morning. Finally, feeling lazy, I put my pen and pad aside and spread myself out on my blanket and quickly went to sleep. I slept for two hours! When I woke, I felt refreshed and recharged and ready to do my writing. If we pay attention, our deeper Self lets us know what we need. If I had been at home, with other people around, the critical voices would have been much more powerful. I would not have allowed myself to be so "lazy" even though my body obviously needed additional rest. Outside, in this place that is particularly special to me, I was able to listen to my inner wisdom and fully enjoy one of my greatest pleasures, a nap on the grass, the breeze caressing my body gently, the birds singing me a lullaby.

---

In our workshops we teach people how to develop an ongoing relationship with nature through mindfulness, reawakening the senses, following intuitions and responding to the invitation of nature. Then we send them out for a solitary walk. With heightened awareness, people become open and receptive to what nature teaches: Things we would ordinarily not give a glance or a passing thought to become imbued with personal meaning.

Rita is a woman in her seventies who has struggled with lifelong self-doubt. She walked down to the beach and in her wandering came across a smooth, egg-shaped stone. Later on, she showed it to the group, describing it as "almost perfect, except for a large indentation on the bottom and a small one on one side. But is perfect," she said, "just as it is, even with its imperfections. Nature is perfect." Her unspoken thought – *"and that means that with my imperfections I am perfect too"* – was understood.

To be who we truly are with our limitations and without criticism or judgment is the most difficult and most important task any one of us can face. Often we choose not to take it on, not even to try because it just seems so impossible. We fight moving forward, taking risks to become more real and instead endure depression, lethargy and loss of soul.

Martha, a woman in her forties, was in just such a crisis when she came to our workshop. External events in her life were forcing her to look at who she really was. She was resisting the inner demand for greater self-awareness and fighting off depression at the same time. When Martha went out for her solitary walk, she stopped to watch a bird in the sky above her. When it flapped its wings against the breeze, it stood still! When it stopped flapping, it would glide with the wind. "Sometimes," she told us afterward, "I guess it takes more effort to stay in one place than it does to move forward."

Dana returned from her hour-long walk with the glow of autumn in her cheeks. She described her walk through the woods, splashing through puddles and kicking leaves with a childlike delight. Down on the beach she found a big rock shaped like a lounge chair and followed the urge to climb into it and sun herself. "I'm 31", she said, " and this is the first time I've ever been alone in this way. I felt like a kid. I had so much fun I felt like I was gone for five minutes!"

None of these experiences are profound. They are a part of the "ordinary magic" of coming to nature with intuition, desire and awareness. Each teaching that people returned with was already there and could have gone unnoticed. But with a different kind of awareness, when we learn to be present, when we reawaken our senses and begin to "see" in a different way, nature will teach us all kinds of things.

Each of us needs to find a way of being more present in nature that fits our own unique way of being. This is part of nature's lesson to be our true Self. Those who are more contemplative might follow the wisdom of Thoreau and "saunter" in nature. Thoreau tells the story of how, during the times of the Crusades, many homeless people wandered aimlessly through towns and villages begging for food and a place to sleep. When asked where they were going, the wanderers would respond, "a la Sainte Terre," to the Holy Land. Recognizing the hypocrisy of this, the village teenagers would taunt these wanderers and call them "Sainte-Terrers," travelers to the Holy Land. From that came "saunterer," meaning anyone who wanders without purpose. Thoreau saw all of nature as the "Holy Land" and described his way of being there as sauntering, wandering aimlessly and at the same time journeying to the Holy Land.[8]

But not everyone wants to saunter. For those who are more active, sauntering would feel boring and drive them crazy. Gerry, for example, does not saunter through nature. He is an avid skier with a deep passion for the sport. He is also a master level instructor. Looking for some exercise in the off-season, Gerry took up mountain biking. What he loves about biking is the action, the challenge of developing the skills, combined with the physical risk involved. He also loves being in the woods and trekking up and down the trails at high speed. But Gerry felt something was missing. When he talked about it, he realized he was out in nature, but not emotionally present there. He was always focusing on his equipment, how his body was responding, or on increasing his skill level. When he rode on Sunday mornings with his biking group, they would periodically stop on a hillside, a beach or in a wooded grove. Rather than responding to the urge they had felt to stop in a particular place and being present in that moment, they would talk about their bikes or their cardiovascular functioning. After our talks, Gerry became more aware of his need to be present, his desire to really stop and respond to these beautiful places of respite. Now when he bikes alone, he opens his senses to the smells, sounds and sights around him. He stops more frequently to experience his surroundings and listen to any inner urging to follow a particular path. And when he is with his biking group he encourages them to do the same.

Sam is a long distance runner. He runs ten miles each day. He has run marathons and many other races, but mostly he runs alone. Sauntering would drive him mad. When he began running, Sam ran mostly on main roads and through the neighborhood streets as so many runners do. But now he runs only on trails through the woods, with all his senses open, deeply present to the beauty and mystery of his surroundings. He tells us that when he runs with his senses fully open and his attention on the experience of himself in nature, he begins to experience himself as a creature among the other creatures darting through the woods. His body is sleek and powerful. He is not separate from all that is around him. In these moments of deep connection to the natural world and to his own "creature nature," Sam feels most fully alive.

❦❦❦

## ❦ Bill

Recently I led a retreat on how nature can help us to be more present to Self, our mate and to God. In the morning, we talked about the things mentioned in this chapter - how nature beckons us, opening our senses, being receptive, responding to the invitation to be present. In the afternoon we went outside to put these things into practice.

The retreat was held at a seminary with 225-acres of open fields, woods and a view of the Long Island Sound only a short distance away. We went outdoors with no specific plan except to listen for the beckoning of nature and to the voice of the Self. We walked in silence for a time, some on the path, some on the grass until one man stopped by a tree and recalled, "When I was ten, Bill, I would've climbed this tree in a minute!" I walked over and, locking my hands together, boosted him to the lowest branch. Soon he was way up in the tree, meowing like a cat and laughing that we would probably have to call the fire department to get him down. Two other men climbed up to join him. We could hear their boyish laughter as the rest of us continued on our walk. Soon, some of the women were climbing trees too, laughing and encouraging the ten-year-old in each other. Later in the day, people recalled the playfulness and spontaneity they had felt as children and remembered experiences in nature that had been exciting, frightening, mysterious or peaceful. On this day, for a little while, they reconnected with that earlier time.

In his essay, "Nature," Emerson wrote that "In the presence of nature a wild delight runs through the man in spite of real sorrows...Crossing a bare Common, in snow puddles, at twilight, under a clouded sky, without having in my thoughts any occurrence of special good fortune, I have enjoyed a perfect exhilaration. I am glad to the brink of fear. In the woods, too, a man casts off his years, as the snake his slough, and at what period soever of life is always a child. In the woods is perpetual youth."[9]

Nature beckons and the child in us responds. Our deeper Self reaches out to nature. We feel it as an urging forth from inside. She invites us, envelops us in her sweet/musky/pungent beauty. We have a moment of communion and a moment of recognition. She is our Mother and our home. We are creatures of her forests and fields. We are her sons and daughter. It is at once magical, mysterious and exhilarating.

38

# SOLITUDE

## 🌺 Jeanne

I am frequently in conflict between my need for human relationships and my longing for solitude. I do not want to be solitary – that is quite different from solitude. For a number of years after my divorce and before settling down with Bill, I was solitary. Those were good and important years, I learned a tremendous amount about myself. I had never been on my own before, having gone from my family into an early marriage. During those solitary years, I found that I was independent, self-sufficient and competent in the world. It felt good to know those things about myself!

In those years without a mate, I also experienced true solitude for, perhaps, the first time in my life. I remember long Sundays when my kids would be with their father and I might not speak to anyone for an entire day. Sometimes I would go down to the river for a walk or to the beach to collect stones. On cold winter days, I would hibernate with only myself, some books and my journal. I would sometimes just contemplate the unusual fact that I had not heard the sound of my own voice in hours! How strange that seemed.

I wrote volumes during those years of solitariness and solitude that came from a desire to know myself fully and deeply. Only by "losing my voice," stopping the constant chatter, was I able to go deep into the silent place inside of me, the place from which we know ourselves.

In the few years since Bill and I have been together, much of our energy has gone to being "in relationship" with each other in ways different from what each of us has known. And while we both have the need and desire to relate deeply, each of us also has a powerful need and desire for solitude. In relationship, our attention is attuned to the other. For our relationships to be meaningful, we must be able to "tune in" to our lover, mate, child or friend. But if we are only attuned to the other, then something in ourselves is left wanting. If I do not know how to tune into myself, to that still, silent place inside, then how can I really attune myself to that place in you? And, if I do not really know that deep place in me, how can you ever really know me deeply? Contrary to what so many of us believe, solitude enhances relationship. And if I value solitude for myself, I will also respect my mate's need for it and not feel threatened or rejected.

It is a bitter-cold weekend in January and I have come to New England alone to find some solitude. I have not had this kind of extended time in a while. At home it seems there are so many things that pull me away from solitude. Someone or something always needs my attention. Some of this is real and some of it is my own projection of how much I am needed by others! In the end, it can all be an excuse not to be with "just only me."

To get into a place of solitude takes time. If I am in the house, the phone rings, begging me to answer, distracting me even if I refuse. One of my sons comes in, usually wanting nothing more than to connect for a moment but "mother energy" fills the home and I am pulled away from myself again. Bill may be around doing his own thing, quite contentedly, but the caretaker in me wants to go and check in on him, or some need in me for nurturing from him surfaces and, again, a chance for solitude is lost in interruptions. Even when no one else is around, I have the house to myself and the pull to be there for others is lessened, "home" gets my attention. I putter around, finish an unfinished task, make soup or clear out old books. I love this time, it is deeply satisfying to the part of me that loves nesting and creating a home. These tasks are not to be devalued. When done mindfully rather than as routine chores, there is a measure of solitude in silently and intently engaging myself in the work of making a home. This is the creative expression of the archetypal energy of the goddess Hestia, the virgin goddess of the hearth and a figure of permanence and stability. Her energy is vitally important in creating a home. However, I long for deep solitude, attached to no other task than to know myself more fully.

So I must leave home and all its pulls to enter into deep solitude. From my talks with other women, my experience is

not unique. The pull of Hestia is powerful and yet a deep part of me yearns to be more fully and completely known. I must leave my nesting tasks for periods of time to respond to that inner urging. The place that most consistently provides the way into that space for me is nature.

The temperature in Western Massachusetts this weekend is only slightly above zero, but I am determined not to let that stop me from a walk at Buffum Falls. I have seen this gently cascading river in early fall and am eager to observe the changes that this frigid cold has wrought. Even on the drive there I am reconnecting to the part of me that loves an adventure. *"I forgot to bring the map - can I find my way without it? Will the back roads be icy? Will I be alone in the woods - will I be scared?"* Already I am entering down into myself by way of my fears.

The woods are lovely, cold, icy, frozen. I must step carefully or I'll slip and fall. I notice many trees and branches fallen since I was last here. I hear a sound and quickly glance behind me. I see nothing. Silence and stillness seem quite quickly to bring up our fears. Perhaps that is why we chatter so much about so little, so that we won't have to go into the silence within and face what we are most afraid of. At the same time, the aspect of solitude I love most is the silencing of my own voice. No need to say anything. And as the voices in my head begin to quiet down, too, a different kind of space opens up inside of me; a space of receptivity and creativity. When I am quiet and in this receptive mode, I can more easily connect to the needs of my deeper Self.

One of the greatest needs is to write. I have wanted to be a writer for a long time, but actually knowing, that deep inside of me, a writer lives and continually awaits my recognition, is a different experience indeed. When I cultivate solitude, when I am quiet and listening, and especially when I am in nature, I open myself to the words, phrases and images that live inside of me.

---

Sandy, a complex and likable woman in her late thirties, has a story very different from mine. Petite and attractive, Sandy initially came to see me because of her obsession with her body image and her compulsive need to exercise. She had been running several miles daily for 15 years and worked out at the gym two or three times a week. Sandy was extremely self-critical and had a mildly distorted body image. While she wanted to slow down and spend more time in quiet meditation, Sandy was terrified of stopping her rigorous routine. Clearly her life was out of balance.

As her story unfolded, the source of Sandy's self-criticism and fear became clear. She remembered vividly her father's harsh and persistent criticism of her mother. Sandy's mother was an obese woman and quite ineffectual in her roles as wife and mother. Hearing her father berate her mother time and time again filled Sandy with the dread that she, too, would someday be an obese and powerless woman. If she stopped running, she'd end up like her mother. While we explored these fears and feelings of inadequacy, I encouraged Sandy to replace some of her running with solitary walks in the miles of woods behind her home. She longed to spend time in her private nature sanctuary in this slowed down way, but feared that if she allowed herself to be quiet her self-critical voices would overwhelm her.

Over time it became apparent to me that Sandy had another fear, too. As our work progressed and she began to feel more comfortable in her body, she realized how dissatisfied she was with her work in the corporate world. Her real desire was to teach movement to other women through dance and exercise. Because of her own struggles with body image, Sandy wanted to be a model for women to feel genuinely comfortable in their bodies. Intuitively, Sandy and I both knew she was powerful with something vital to teach other women, but she had had no model for this. Her own mother was big but not powerful. How, then, could Sandy accept herself as a powerful woman? Perhaps, too, that was part of her fear of going into solitude in the woods. If she were to be in nature – surrounded by a big, powerful Mother! – in a meditative way, Sandy would finally have to face her self-critical voices and her fears directly, and accept her own power as a woman.

After many months of working through her false beliefs about herself and making some important changes, Sandy made a significant breakthrough. She came to her session and described her experience in this way:

> I didn't run this week at all! Instead I had the most extraordinary walks in the woods! It was like a winter wonderland. There was a light dusting of snow on the ground and the trees. Everything was so still. I saw things around me in a way I never have before. And I began to cry when I realized how good it felt to be with myself in this way – I wasn't running or doing or worrying about whether or not I was going to put on weight because I wasn't running. I was just walking and being quiet and being with myself. I've never felt that before. It felt so good!

Sandy continued her slowed-down routine for several weeks, during which time she also did more meditation and journaling. Then she resumed her running. However, the respite from her normally very rigorous routine seemed to help her in several ways. For one, solitude was now a possibility for Sandy. She found that she could be still, that nothing bad happened, that, in fact, she felt good being with herself in that way. She also became significantly less fearful of teaching. Opportunities to teach dance and exercise classes began, synchronistically, to open up for her and she courageously accepted the challenges. Finally, as Sandy developed a greater acceptance of her own path as an active, body-oriented way, her obsession with her weight diminished. She also understood that the need for solitude did not mean giving up her active ways, but that to have periods of lessened activity and increased receptivity was a way for her to stay connected to her inner voice and the path of her deeper Self.

Though it is bitter cold in the woods this day, I am dressed warmly and only my fingers feel cold. I stop along the rocky slope leading down to a lake and look for a spot in which I can do a short meditation. How being in nature enhances that time of stillness! I do not want to miss an opportunity. I look around for a place to sit but the day is cloudy and everything looks so cold. In a moment, the sun slips out from behind a cloud, shining warmly on a number of choice rocks. I choose one. Perfect. In frigid cold I am warmed by the sun.

In the woods, at the river or in an open field, these are the places where I cultivate solitude. These are the places that open me to where the writer lives deep inside. I do not always connect with that part of myself immediately. The effects of solitude are cumulative and we need to build stamina for it a little at a time. Solitude is a state of being that needs to be cultivated regularly, just as the gardener continually cultivates the ground in which she plants her seeds. But even before planting, she must clear the weeds and debris that choke the land. In the same way, we must understand what might block us from going into solitude and cultivating the deep, creative parts of ourselves.

Past experiences always have an impact on what we do now. Many of us have painful memories, often repressed, of feelings of fear, emptiness, isolation, rejection, or not belonging associated with being alone. Our friend, Ben, recently went on a vision quest in a wooded area a short distance from his home. By nature Ben is an extroverted, gregarious man. He loves to move around and talks with everyone. To be in deep solitude for 48 hours brought up his most fundamental fears.

Ben was an only child and spent long hours in isolation. He tried to ward off the pain of this intense insolation by engaging in activity. Through his own therapy, he had done much grieving for his childhood losses, but the vision quest required him to face once again his deepest fear of being alone, out of contact with other people. At first, Ben managed to avoid "sitting still and just being" by puttering around his small space and cleaning up. He had a very clean space! But eventually a steady downpour forced him into his tent. In this even smaller space, Ben felt trapped; he couldn't move for hours. Forced into stillness, he began journaling and meditating. He grieved again the losses of childhood and other profound losses in his life. After a period of time, a shift took place in Ben. He wrote poetry and began to connect to the deep desire to do more spiritual work with men.

After his vision quest, Ben felt an increased longing for regular periods of solitude. A few months later he took a ten-day, solo motorcycle trip to Nova Scotia with the conscious intent to be in silence as much of the time as possible. He returned with a commitment to himself to more fully embrace his own power as a man and pursue the spiritual work he wants to do with other men.

For Greg, a vigorous man in his mid-thirties, solitude is associated with terror and the black hole of emptiness. He wonders why he has to be doing something all the time; why he can't just hang out with himself. Like Ben, he is extroverted but longs for solitude. Greg's parents were divorced when he was quite young. He and his two sisters lived with their father and would visit their drug-addicted mother on weekends. Greg's father worked two jobs and was rarely home, so he and his sisters would do what they could to keep busy until he finally arrived home late in the evening. Depressed and despairing, Greg became overweight and felt like an outcast among his peers. Finally, at 16 years old, unable to cope any longer with his profound feelings of emptiness and isolation, Greg took the family car one night and had a near-fatal accident. Frightened of ever re-experiencing that state of intense despair, he avoids anything he feels might bring him to the edge of that abyss. Solitude terrifies him.

People avoid solitude for other reasons, too. Oftentimes, it is associated with "badness" - "An idle mind is the devil's workshop". Some patients relate stories of parents who would bang on their bedroom door asking "What are you doing in there!?" Other parents even went so far as to remove the door from a child's room! The unspoken, but loud and clear, message in this is that we might do something "bad" if we're alone.

Adolescence is often a time of life with long periods of brooding, self-critical introspection. Finding no peer group with whom they fit, many teenagers feel isolated. On the outside they are intensely critical of the adult world, but it is really when they look inward that they are most critical. While most of us block out the memory of that uncomfortable period of life, on some level of consciousness it is remembered and hinders us from entering into solitude for fear that those feelings of intense self-criticism will be rekindled.

Often in these earlier times of life, isolation and solitude were forced on us by life circumstances. Or, time alone was forbidden to us. We felt powerless in these situations. In contrast, actively choosing solitude as a vital part of our psychospiritual journey is empowering. Since it is not a familiar experience for most of us, we need to approach periods of solitude a little at a time and build up stamina for longer periods of solitude. It's like learning to swim: you don't go out into the deep water the first time, but ease in gradually from the shore.

Solitude begins as we slowly muddle through the layers of "stuff" that become the pathway to our deeper Self. For me, waiting somewhere down that path is the writer. For Bill, it is the teacher. For Sandy, it is the dancer. Solitude is a tool to help each of us connect to this deeper part of Self.

Most of my writing comes either during or after a trek into nature. I always try to have a small notebook or paper and pen tucked in a pocket when I go outside. When I am open and receptive, thoughts, words and images come to mind and they can be quickly lost. It's like waking from a dream in the dark of night. We're sure we'll remember every vivid detail, only to wake in the morning with a hazy memory that we had a very significant dream during the night. Numbers of times I have wandered off into the woods or down to the river and neglected to take pen and paper with me. A poem, a deep insight or an opening sentence for an essay comes up from that open space and I spend my entire walk repeating the poem or the sentence over and over in my head, trying not to lose it. In the meantime, I have lost the beauty and the solitude of my walk. When I can write down the thought, I can then put it aside and be more fully present to myself and nature.

***

It is the first day of February, cold, but not as cold as it could be. Two weeks ago I was in New England. Today, I am at the ocean, a 25-minute drive from our home. Bill and my sons, Chris and John, are all off doing their own things. This is an opportunity for me to go off and be with myself.

The sun sparkles on the foaming, frantically crashing waves. Their constant, dull roar at first disconcerts me. It is a full half hour into my walk before I begin to re-enter my body. Before that I am distracted by my mind: random, wandering thoughts, a song replaying over and again. The colors of the shells and stones divert my attention. I choose a few and tuck them carefully into my pocket. My ears begin to ache from the chill winter wind. Gradually, I become aware of my breathing. How good it feels to take a breath deep into my body! I imagine it flows all the way down to my feet. I begin to feel my feet on the ground, each crunch of my steps in the sand. Breathing in, I feel myself in my body. How good it feels! How happy and grateful I am in this moment to have my body so I can experience this day in this way. My ears no longer ache.

In fact, the day no longer feels cold even though the wind still blows. I am aware that as I continue to pay attention to my breathing, I become more and more conscious of how it feels to be in my body. Each breath seems to be pulled down through my lungs, into my belly, my womb, through my groin, down through my legs and into the earth. I feel the weight of myself, the muscles in my thighs as I take each step. I feel sensual, alive. My thoughts drift to how much more connected I am to my sensuality when I spend time in nature. I like feeling this sensuality totally contained in myself, in my solitude, with no urge to act on the feeling, but just to stay present to me in my own body. Virgin sensuality.

I often talk with my women patients about the idea of being a "virgin." We have been so misled about what it means to be a virgin. Most women, especially those who have been abused at some time in their life, are intrigued by the idea of being "re-virginized." Years ago my own therapist introduced me to this idea. It has helped me over and over again through the years with myself and in my work with other women. In its original meaning, a virgin is simply a "young woman" or a woman who is unwed. Early usage of the term virgin had nothing to do with a woman's chastity or sexual innocence, but referred only to her marital status. M. Esther Harding, a Jungian analyst, interprets the religious use of the concept of virgin as symbolic, referring to "a quality, to a subjective state, a psychological attitude, not to a physiological or external fact." A virgin, she continues, is a woman who "belongs to herself alone, she is 'one-in-herself.'" A virgin is neither compelled to be chaste nor to "yield to an unwanted embrace."[10]

This concept is so vitally important for women. To belong to no man or woman, spouse, parent or child, but to belong only to herself. If I am virgin, I give myself to no other, sexually or otherwise, unless it is my choice to do so. How deeply we must go inside ourselves to find this "virgin Self." I tell women that as they begin to connect to their deep Self, as they no longer allow themselves to be at the whim of the needs of others, they are being "re-virginized," possessed only by themselves. We must have periods of solitude to reclaim ourselves. In ancient times, and in traditional cultures, women had regular periods of solitude. At the time of their bleeding, when they were "in their moon time," women would leave the men and children and go off together to the "menstrual hut." Here they would not cook, tend the land or perform any of their usual tasks. The time was spent alone, fasting and performing other rites of purification. It was a time of introversion, a time to connect with the deep instinctual Self. I also like to imagine that it was a time for the women to just take care of each other, to laugh and be playful, to tell stories and share the mysteries of being a woman.

Today, when we are bleeding, women continue with their normal routine as if nothing is different. We go to work, care for children and mates, cook meals, take care of the home. We make no time for seclusion or solitude, no time to be still and introspective, no time to be with other women who are bleeding, no time to honor the cyclical nature of our lives. Life goes on as if nothing has changed. But we are changed during our moon time. We are different. Ask any man who is with a bleeding woman. If he knows his woman, he knows when her moon time is approaching. Our moods change, we may become intensely sexual, or distant and irritable; our physical and mental stamina may decline; we may feel physiologically and psychologically out of balance. We refer to this natural process, men and women alike, in disparaging terms: bleeding is "the curse;" we are "wearing the rag," etc. Harding traces the physical ills now commonly associated with bleeding to the discarding of traditional practices of seclusion during menstruation. Perhaps the negative ways in which we talk about bleeding are really an expression of the unconscious anger that we feel because we no longer honor our natural feminine rhythms. Perhaps our bodies are telling us we need to return to this time of regular solitude.

When I talk with my women patients about this, I encourage them to create their own menstrual hut. Perhaps that is a warm bath with candles and incense burning, or some time under the covers with a good book to read, a journal to write in, or just for some extra rest. It could be a lawn chair in the sun at the beach or in the backyard. No disturbances, no tasks, if only for half an hour. Just this small act gives an important and powerful message to our deeper Self that we value ourselves, that we recognize the cyclical nature of life as it is for women, and that we are trying to honor our natural way of being in the world.

❧

The constant sounding of the waves that, at first, was disconcerting now lulls me. The sound is soothing and seems also to ground me in my body. I must be in my body to be "virgin." My body must belong to me if I am to be "one-in-myself." Nature reconnects me to my body, to my deeper Self, again and again.

❦

Last night, as I thought about having a walk today, the image of open meadows swept silently into my mind. "Ah! yes, the meadows. I will go there tomorrow." Now as I walk, feeling the breeze on my face and my feet on the ground, I orient myself to the outside world. How grand these trees are! How I love the rich, textured brown of their aging skin. I am sure they have been here a long time. I see the path to the meadows veering off to my right. "Here's my path, " I say to myself, "my path to my meadows." In my solitude I ponder my possessiveness. At first, I think it is pure Western materialism. I cannot just *be* in the meadow, I must possess the meadow. The meadow is mine. Plowing more deeply, though, I think, perhaps, it is not so much having the meadow for my own as it is searching for a place, seeking to belong. I vacillate. There are fresh footprints on my path. They may come, these others, but not while I am here, please. I want the meadow to myself. I have come here for solitude and I am Self-ish in this.

Standing at the edge of her - this meadow is so abundantly feminine - a pang, an ache grips my breath for only a moment. How beautiful! She is spread out before me, silent, steadfast, inviting. This beauty touches me and like a lover I enter, longing to know each gently rising curve of her, each nook and cranny, each softly sloping hollow, each blade of yellowed, green grass. Sweet meadow grass brushes my senses and is gone. But it wakes me and whispers to me in one

53

split second of the wild abandon and the fecundity of spring. A promise as winter lingers on.

My steps are light. I want to run and twirl and dance. A memory slips in of my "dancing field." Years ago I had images of myself dancing in a field of tall grass, high on top of a cliff overlooking the sea. In the imagery, I was always barefoot and wearing a light cotton sun dress. I would dance in the midst of the tall grass and feel the wind caress my body. Sometimes I would slip my dress over my head and dance naked. I felt so free! Over time, as I allowed the imagery to have a life of its own, it changed and evolved. I would sometimes meet a "Wise Old Man" there. I would ask him questions about myself and he would answer me, often silently, guiding me gently and wisely. When I felt sad and despairing, I would climb into his lap like a little girl and he would stroke my hair and comfort me. Sometimes I would see my "Earth Mother" in the field. I loved her freedom to be fully a woman, to be alive, sensual, and joyful in her womanness. She taught me about that same woman in myself.

One day, I went into my dancing field imagery, looked around and noticed how small the field was. How had I never noticed that before? The Wise Old Man was there. When I asked him about it, he told me it was time to venture out of this field, to see what lay beyond these boundaries. I was angry and didn't want to go. I was afraid and began to cry. He just smiled tenderly at me and gently touched my arm. In time, the imagery changed and I did venture out, little by little, down a path, through a woods, eventually coming to the edge of a mountain overlooking valleys and hills that finally reached a vast ocean. After that the imagery stopped.

Now and then, I think about that imagery. It had a profound effect on me. Over time I came to understand it as a motion picture of my psyche. The field was an image of my real Self, the place where I was most free and most true. As my true Self came more out into the world, the field became too small and I had to move beyond its limitations. When the imagery no longer served me intrapsychically, it stopped and other things took its place.

Here, in the meadow, I feel the same kind of aliveness and expansiveness that I felt in my dancing field imagery. Sitting on a fence in silent reverie, first two hawks, then four, glide overhead. I am suddenly struck with an urgent love

for this place, for the meadow meandering before me, for the circling hawks, and for the placid blue sky arching high above us all. "I love you," I say aloud. "I love you, hawks! I love you, meadow! I love you, beautiful, beautiful blue sky!" This love feels so pure, so unencumbered. I want nothing but to be here. In this solitude, in this place of separation from the "real world," I know it is not really the meadow I want to possess but my deeper Self. My true Self.

⁂

In silence and solitude, just sitting, just being, connects us to some inner place of non-intellectual "knowing" that is, as Rabbi David Cooper says, our basic nature.[11] Here there is peace and love. Beneath the constant outer noise of the world and the constant inner chatter of worry about money, sadness of loss or emptiness, self-criticism, is the peace that underlies all things. Mostly we can connect with it only for moments at a time. Without periods of solitude, we cannot connect at all.

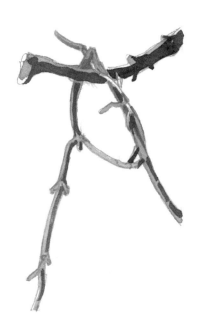

# CARETAKERS

So many of us are caretakers. We work all day in caretaker professions such as psychotherapists, nurses, teachers, massage therapists or ministers. Or, we are natural caretakers, the ones friends and family come to for help. We are always there for others when they need us, readily offering support, consolation, guidance, a listening ear, a meal, money, a ride – whatever is needed.

Caretakers struggle with two things: taking care of ourselves and letting others take care of us. Invariably we have trouble saying no to others in need and inevitably we become depleted and worn out from being needed so much. We give until we have nothing left. And then we collapse. We nourish others but receive little or no nurturing for ourselves. If we don't do the psychological work needed to bring ourselves into balance, eventually our bodies force us to stop our caretaking. We become sick or we can't get out of bed and have to sleep all day.

Nancy, a woman in her mid-forties, is so busy trying to keep things together for her husband and grown sons that her own life is in utter chaos. Last winter, she was out of work sick for several days. When a colleague asked what had happened, Nancy told her she had been laid up with the flu. Her friend was extremely sympathetic since the flu that year had been a particularly bad one. Nancy surprised her with her response. "Are you kidding? Those were the best three days I've had in years. All I did was lie in bed and vomit and sleep. I couldn't do a thing for anyone else!"

While we can laugh at the humorous side of this exchange, it's sad that Nancy had to wait for her body to break down to get the rest she so desperately needed. But this is a typical scenario for the caretaker. We keep going and going until some outside force knocks us down. When others ask us how we're doing we usually tell them "fine, "great," "couldn't be better." Even though we are depressed, tired or anxious, we are unable to admit this to others and, most often, to ourselves. We easily see and respond to the needs of others, but so rarely see that we have the same needs. Even when we do see them, rarely are we able to express these needs and let others take care of us. Yet, secretly, we wish that someone would do for us what we so willingly do for them.

<hr />

At our workshops for caretakers, we lead participants in a guided imagery exercise to help them connect with when and how they first became caretakers. Many of them are surprised at how early they began this life pattern. Sometimes children are given this role.

For example, Margie was ten when her father died. She and her brother were left to take care of their manic-depressive mother and a blind aunt who lived with them. Margie marks that time as the end of her childhood.

When Dana was nine, her father held a gun to her mother's head and threatened to kill her. Dana had to get her younger brother out of the house and call the police from a neighbor's house. From then on, Dana remembers, she was the grownup, competent, responsible one in the family.

At the age of two, Karen remembers being in her crib with her sickly twin sister and her mother coming in and saying, "Take care of your sister, Karen." She has been taking care of her ever since.

Some children intuitively sense that a family member needs them and they assume the role of their caretaker. Kelly remembers when her musician father would leave for weeks at a time to perform on cruise ships. Her mother would lie in bed crying and Kelly would climb in next to her and massage her back. It's no surprise that in her twenties Kelly became a massage therapist.

When Jack was ten, his alcoholic father committed suicide. He was left with an alcoholic mother who then remarried another alcoholic. Jack becomes enraged when he talks about his childhood spent protecting his mother.

Tony was always a good kid and high achiever. As a boy, he was constantly arguing his father's or his brother's cause with his mother. He continues this childhood role in his work now as an attorney.

As we can see in these families, death, divorce, illness or some other crisis often pushes a child into the caretaker role. He or she becomes a small adult, overly responsible, competent and "good." In other families, the role evolves in a different way.

Pat, for instance, greatly admired her caretaker mother, and from the time she was small, wanted to be just like her. She, then, became a caretaker through the process of identification.

While these are some of the ways that the pattern of caretaking begins, it is then reinforced by the praise and status the caretaking child receives. She is told how "mature" and "grown up" she is. He is told how "good," "responsible" and "adult" he is. Since all children hunger for approval, and in many of these homes that needed affirmation is in short supply, the child continues more and more of the caretaking behavior that he knows will provide that form of approval. The role of caretaker then becomes the main source of feelings of self-worth and pride. Indeed, when we work with a caretaker in psychotherapy and begin to encourage him or her to let go of some of the caretaking, invariably the person becomes anxious. Their deep fear is that, if they let go of this source of self-worth, where will the self-esteem come from? "Will people still like me? Will they think that I'm selfish?" These are the questions caretakers ask. So much of the sense of Self has become invested in the good feelings that emanate from this role that the pattern becomes well entrenched. "It makes me feel good about myself," the caretakers say, "when I do something for someone else."

The healing journey of the caretaker comes about from learning to take care of ourselves and allowing others to take care of us. This does not mean no longer taking care of others, but rather knowing the limits of our own physical, psychological and emotional energy and taking in nourishment from others in equal doses to the nourishment we give out. The caretaker's Golden Rule might be, *Let others do for me what I do for others*. Again, since so much of self is invested in the caretaker role, to follow this rule is no easy task.

In our work with caretakers, we talk about going to nature for help in this healing process. Nature is our Mother. If we have a warm, intimate relationship with nature, we are able to receive the nourishing mothering that she has to offer. While we all need this kind of parenting, this is especially true for caretakers. Because our mothers and fathers frequently were too depressed, frightened, overwhelmed, unavailable or needy, they were often unable to give the emotional nourishment we really needed. As a result, there is an inner emptiness that we try to fill with food, drink, work and other addictions, or by taking care of others. What is most needed is to find additional sources of parenting and allow these sources to fill the emptiness. We can do this through relationships with friends, aunts, uncles, grandparents, mentors, therapists and others. Often we need to work through our blocks to seeking out and being receptive to these human sources of nourishment. But nurturing doesn't only come from other people. One of the greatest and most dependable sources of nourishment is nature.

When we talk with our caretaker patients about this, we suggest that they find a special place in nature where there is an intuitive feeling of at homeness. Just as deer are at home in the woods, dolphins in the sea, and hawks in the sky, each of us human creatures has a particular place in nature where we have a sense of deep belonging. There we feel more at peace, more free, closer to our true Self, more fully human and alive. For some of us, it is the woods, for others the ocean, still others feel most at home along rivers, in meadows, deserts or mountains. Some of us already know where our home is, but others need to visit various nature places and listen for our inner responses to those places. When a place beckons, we need to follow, trusting our intuitive sense of a place where we feel at home.

We recommend to caretakers, as we recommend to others, that the time spent in nature be spent alone. It is the well-ingrained trait of caretakers that whenever we are in the presence of another we tend to think of that person's needs before our own. It's part of the pattern. For a caretaker to be walking in the woods or strolling along the beach with another, even if that other is a lover or best friend, some version of the following inner dialogue will be occurring: "Is he having a good time? Does she really like this? Would he like to walk faster...slower...sit down...stop now...talk...do something else...walk up that path...collect beach rocks?" And on and on. The inner concern about the other interferes with caretakers getting the nourishment they need for themselves.

Being alone also quiets down our projective processes. Whenever we are in the presence of another, at some level of consciousness we are projecting our own inner "stuff" onto the other. Since caretakers generally tend to be self-critical with high expectations and many "shoulds," we will project these onto our companion - no matter how good a friend or lover the other is. As we walk in the woods, along the beach, or up a hillside, we will be wondering what he or she will think of us if we want to...walk without talking...jump in the water...gather sea shells...climb atop the rocks...take a nap in the meadow grass. This will inhibit us and close us down. To quiet these projective processes it is better, at least initially, to travel alone.

---

## 🌸 Bill

Max, a minister in his fifties, was weary and depleted from many months of taking care of the needs of his parishioners with little respite. Responding to my encouragement to take better care of himself, Max began to take periodic long walks alone in the woods. At the end of these sylvan sojourns, he felt nourished and recharged. He understood finally what I had explained to him about the flow of energy. How energy flows from a high source to a low source. Max is a high-energy source. When his depleted, low-energy parishioners came for pastoral counseling they left feeling lighter and recharged. Max, however, felt drained because he did not take regular care of his own need to be replenished, either by spending time with nurturing people or by going into nature. As Max spent more time in the woods and began to allow nature's energy to fill him on a regular basis, he felt less depleted and more in touch with is own need for nurturing.

One wintry morning, Max was walking in a local wildlife sanctuary. He had begun to go there regularly and felt this place to be a true sanctuary, a place of psychological and spiritual renewal. This particular morning was bitter cold, yet Max had set aside this time for himself and would not be deterred by the weather. Caretakers are often persistent in spite of difficulties, and today Max was grateful for that trait. Frequently on these woodland walks, Max would spontaneously start chanting. This day was no different. Sometimes strange, guttural sounds would emanate from deep within his chest, sounds that reminded him of the chanting of Tibetan monks from Gyuto monastery. On other occasions, the chant would be some repeated word or phrase. With my encouragement to trust his own process, Max has ceased to be uncomfortable with these experiences and had come to know the chants as "soul soundings." On this day, the phrase that flowed through him was "I hunger for your love." This was familiar, he had chanted these words several times before in these woods. They reflected, he felt, his soul's longing to be more connected to God's love.

After walking for about a half hour, Max began to feel the cold. Suddenly he felt the sun streaming down on him through an opening in the gray, winter sky. How warm it felt! He closed his eyes and imagined, as he often did, the sun as a manifestation of God's love. But this day he felt a difference. The warmth he felt was a feminine warmth, mother's love rather than father's; love emanating from the Divine Feminine. He felt this in the totality of his being.

In a moment, Max was flooded with free floating images of mothering while the words "mom, momma, mommy" reverberated in his mind. In the first image, he was a baby contentedly nestled against the breasts of a warm and welcome mother. Next, he was an infant securely tucked in the papoose on an Indian mother's back. This image struck Max in an especially powerful way. Oftentimes on Monday mornings, he would get an image of himself strapping a heavy pack onto his back, a symbol of how burdensome his work often felt, especially at the beginning of a new week. To experience himself being carried on a mother's strong shoulders was a significant reversal of his image of burden. In the next image, Max was a frightened young boy holding

tight to a mother's legs, his head resting against her as she reassured him that "everything will be fine, Mommy's here." As he was cradled in these images Max suddenly became aware of just how little mothering he had received from his own mother. She was too frightened and preoccupied with the everyday struggles of coping with his gambling father to be available to Max emotionally. Finally, standing among the trees in the warm sun, Max felt himself rocked in a mother's arms, swaying back and forth as she sang a lullaby. How soothing and nurturing it felt to give himself over freely to those powerful images of mothering.

In this kind of imagery state, time is experienced in a totally different way than we usually experience it. Indeed, there is a sense of no time or of eternal time. When Max emerged from his reverie and returned to his car, he found he had been in that spot in the bitter cold woods, for at least two hours. And he did not feel cold at all. In fact, he felt deeply warmed by the Mother love that he had received. For fifty years, Max now knew, he had "hungered" for this kind of love. On this chilly winter morning in the woods, nature had created an opening for him to receive the nurturing and mothering that he so badly needed. At last he had a source that was always available to him for some of the maternal nourishment he had unconsciously craved all his life.

Another central issue for caretakers is the need for real family. The yearning for family is innately human, coming from deep within our heart and soul. A real family provides a sense of connection, nurturing and sustaining love. A place where we are free to be ourselves and where we feel a sense of at homeness. Of course, there are still conflicts, disappointments and times of "muddling through" even in the most nurturing family.

Some of us are fortunate that our biological family meets our "real" family needs. Unfortunately many of us, especially caretakers, do not feel that way. Whenever we go to our family to get emotional needs met, the old, unresolved conflicts arise. Yet we continue to go back partially because of the "shoulds," the sense of obligation and loyalty. On a deeper level we go in the hope that this time it will be different. This time it will be a real family. Inevitably, we are disappointed.

As we develop psychologically, get more in touch with our own needs and begin to reclaim who we really are, there is a natural distancing from family in order to see them in a more realistic way. We feel sadness, anger, grief, guilt and tremendous loss as we realize that our family could not fulfill all of our childhood needs for love, affirmation, protection and encouragement to be who we really are. As long as we hold onto the child's wish for that kind of fulfillment and keep going back to the same people to get what they cannot give us, we will be eternally disappointed.

In our work, not only with caretakers but especially with them, we encourage this psychological distancing from family in order to get a clearer perspective on what needs can realistically be met by them. We also encourage people to begin to find what we call a real or emotional family. This family consists of friends who can be there when we really need them, listen to us in a non-judgmental way and also challenge us in areas in which we need to grow. People who can laugh, play and have fun with us, who can be our emotional brothers and sisters. Older people may become emotional parents who can affirm us, guide us in life decisions, and be role models in ways our own parents could not. In other cultures, the idea of family extends beyond the immediate family into which one is born. In the Jewish kibbutz and in native or tribal cultures, children are raised communally. A child has many parents, many brothers and sisters. The tasks of nurturing a child physically, mentally and emotionally are shared. No wonder we often feel our families have failed us in some way when the demand to provide so much is left to so few.

Gwen, a guidance counselor in a high school, is a caretaker. She just turned forty. Traditionally she has spent her birthday with her parents and two brothers. Gwen would go to these gatherings with a mixture of dread and hopeful anticipation. "This time will be different," she would think. Invariably her alcoholic brother would drink too much and start an argument. Even on those occasions when he failed to come, the conversation inevitably wound around to the latest crisis in his life. It was Gwen's birthday, but her brother always seemed to be the center of attention. Not even this one day a year could she feel important and special.

This year, with much angst, Gwen decided to do something different. She called six of her women friends and invited them to share her birthday by having dinner at her favorite Italian restaurant. Because of a lifetime of disappointments with her family, Gwen was sure they wouldn't be able to go, or that they would prefer to do something with someone else. But everyone did come. To her surprise Gwen had the best birthday ever! Her friends toasted her, telling her they were glad she was born, glad she was in their lives. Over time, as Gwen was able to take in this emotional nourishment from her friends, she felt more and more a sense of "real" family. Her relationship with her biological family improved, as often happens, as she stopped going to them for emotional nourishment that they were unable to give. Needs that they, for many reasons, could not fill could now be filled by her "sisters."

Another source of family for caretakers (and everyone else) is nature. Indigenous cultures the world over, including the early European cultures, have always known nature as family, but we have forgotten that part of our family tree! The stories remain, however, passed down from generation to generation to remind us "from whence we came." Black Elk told us that "with all beings and all things we shall be as relatives." The "two-legged" and "four-legged" and "winged ones" are family in Native American cultures.[12] Stories from the East tell us that the disciples of Buddha were taught to be compassionate toward and in relationship with all sentient beings. Hindu theology teaches that the supreme being was incarnated in the form of various species and, thus, the creatures of nature must be related to accordingly.

European lore connects us to stories of our "ancestral trees." In Scandinavia the legend goes that the first man was created from an ash tree and the first woman from an elm. The

Celts have a similar legend. The mythology of many cultures provides stories like these, of human beings descending from trees, while others tell of the souls of ancestors that reside in the trees after death. In the Christian tradition, St. Francis related to trees as "living relatives, like grandparents, uncles, and aunts."[13] He taught that all aspects of creation – the sun, the moon, the winds – are members of our family. We are surrounded, it seems, by "all our relations."

## 🌸 Bill

As my relationship with nature has deepened over the last four or five years, I have experienced a growing connection to the other creatures as family. The great pine trees in the woods nearby have become "mother" and "father" trees. The welcoming of their outstretched branches, the reliable strength of their trunks and the hard-to-describe sense that they are there for me when I need them has helped to fill a lifelong need for parenting. A clue to the depth of my connection to my tree family is the image I often have of myself as a tree that walks around. The crows are my "brothers." Each morning they sit in the tree outside the kitchen door waiting to see what leftovers from last night's meal I will put out for them. I observe their sense of community, delight in their playfulness and defend them to others who perceive them only as annoying, noisy pests. In my office, I have a pair of crow wings that were a gift from a shaman friend of mine. When patients ask about them, I tell them about my love for crows hoping that one day they, too, will develop a relationship with my brothers.

In my walks in the woods, a chipmunk will dart across the path and my usual spontaneous response is "Hi, little one!" The wind rustles through the trees and I say to myself, "Sister Breeze is coming by." As I saunter along, duality drops and I touch the bushes and branches, stick my nose into the flowers, rub the tree trunks and smile a lot. I feel a sense of being at home with this family. I am reawakened to our long-dormant ancestral connection. As my relationship with nature develops, I feel an increased desire to spend more time with my extended family. Sometimes I find it difficult to leave them and return to the madness of everyday life. Yet, as with any visit to a real family, I carry their presence and sustaining nourishment with me as I walk through my day.

---

For most of us caretakers our parents were not a reliable source of emotional nourishment, consolation or presence when we needed them. Because of their own depression, fearfulness, addiction, self-absorption or economic survival needs, they were either rarely or inconsistently available. As a result, most caretakers learn at an early age that adults are undependable and the only person they can really rely on is themselves. Or they unconsciously depend on some substance they can give to themselves - food, alcohol or even God. Jeanne and I learned from our experiences that nature is another source of nourishment that is reliable, trustworthy, ever present and waiting for us when we need her. Each time we visit her waters, woods, meadows or hills, we return replenished, energized, quieted down and feeling less alone. We gradually learn that we can rely on nature to nourish us as we nourish others. We begin to internalize the knowledge that we are not alone, that we, too, need taking care of, and we become more able to ask for that nurturing in our other relationships. And, nature is always there, always beckoning us to pay her a visit and receive the nourishment she has to give.

# Intimacy

Solitary time in nature is important, as we have said, especially when initially venturing outdoors in a more conscious way. Projection of our internal "stuff" is diminished, we are less critical and judgmental of ourselves and we can begin to be more present and experience more of our true Self. But nature is also a beautiful place to be present with one's mate. We think of ourselves as mated, just as the other creatures of nature mate, whether for a lifetime as the wolves and swans do or for a season as the foxes do. For whatever time there is for us to be together, we are mated. When we are in nature together and allowing ourselves to be present to her and to each other, we feel that matedness even more powerfully.

Whether it is the woods we love, or open meadows, the mountains, or the ocean, being with one's mate in a special place in nature can help us to learn about each other and about intimacy in a relationship. We hear so much about intimacy these days, about how women want intimacy and about how men fear intimacy. But do we really know what it means to be intimate? Oftentimes when we talk with patients about intimacy in their relationships they will tell us about their sexual relationship. Many people seem to understand intimate to mean sexual. While sexual intimacy is certainly one kind of intimacy, to be sexual with someone does not necessarily mean we are being intimate.

The word *intimate* derives from the superlative form of the Latin word *inter* which means within. The superlative of within, Thomas Moore explains in *Soul Mates*, can be translated as "most within." "Intimacy," Moore explains, "means living in the "very within" place of the relationship; it means looking into and beneath the surfaces."[14] So to be intimate with someone means, literally, to know the most within places of that person. This is so profound a way of looking at intimacy that it needs elaboration. How many of us feel that our partner really knows our most within? To what extent do we know each other's fantasies and fears, hopes and dreads? Do we know each other's history? Do we know the other's darkness and silliness, the other's image of God or philosophy of life? When we allow the other deep within us, to know our most secret, tender and vulnerable places, and when the other allows us to know them in the same way, then our relationship is an intimate one.

We are all longing for and searching for intimacy. So what makes it so difficult to allow another into that most within place? Our deeper Self is dormant or suppressed because of what happened to us when we were more open. As children we were simple and uncomplicated, our most within parts were right out in the world. But along the way we were wounded, often unwittingly, by adults who felt it best that certain aspects of our child-self be kept under control or banished from the world altogether. Or, we were physically or sexually abused. Or, we were wounded by the humiliating comments of childhood and adolescent peers, teachers, relatives or other adults. For some of us, the inner Self was not so much wounded, but rather treated as unimportant, so that the Self has withered and dried up for lack of nourishment. School achievement, athletic ability, doing household chores and other skills necessary for survival in our secular world were treated as important but the inner Self was undernourished or totally neglected. Each time a part of our child-self was wounded, whether it was our sense of playfulness, our intelligence, our anger, our creativity, our fearfulness, our sexuality, we buried it deep down in the shadows of our psyche. Some parts of Self we forgot about totally; others we had to exert tremendous psychic energy to keep at bay. As adults, these "shadow" aspects of Self become, in effect, our most within. This is the part of Self that we begin to know as we go into nature alone. These are also the parts of Self that we must allow our mate to know and must know in our mate if we are to be truly intimate.

Intimacy is both wonderful and terrifying. The wonderful part comes from the deep, human desire to be known and accepted for who we are. Those moments when another knows and accepts us are magical, soul-making and heart warming. The terrifying part is the fear that we will be rejected. We project that, since our parents, teachers, adolescent friends, past lovers or others disapproved of certain aspects of our Self, then other people, including our mate, will also disapprove. In fact, we believe that our mate more than anyone else will dislike our shadow parts. In this relationship more than any other, we project early childhood experiences with our parents and peers. So we are frightened that if we show our deeper Self, we will again be rejected.

Daily living provides us with so many distractions that we need never be intimate. We tend to work, to children, to our homes, to friends and family and often end up with little time or energy for the person with whom we most want to be. Couples complain that they have so little time together, that the tasks of everyday life are so demanding and depleting, there is little time left for each other. And when we do have the time, we are so exhausted or cranky that the quality of that time is not good. Working overtime just to pay bills, the demands of raising children, taking care of a home, commitments to relatives, friends and community leave us enough energy, perhaps, to watch some TV, rent a video or go out for a quick bite to eat at a fast food place. Quality time together? What's that? With so little time to really talk with and listen to each other, couples often find out the details of each other's lives quite by accident, a chance remark at dinner or a telephone conversation overheard. When one partner says to the other, "You never told me that," the other replies, "Who had time? We were so busy with the kids and talking about where we're going to get the money to pay the car insurance that I forgot to tell you." This is a tragedy. "Each of us needs to withdraw," Maya Angelou tells us, "from the cares which will not withdraw from us. We need hours of aimless wandering or spates of time sitting on park benches..."[15] We would be wise to heed these words individually and as couples. What we most want, intimacy, we give the least time and importance.

## 🌸 Bill

Some couples, at least, know that this lack of time and attention given to each other is a problem. But others are almost totally unaware of the need for time together to get to know the most within of the other. A man recently came to see me because he was suffering with intense anxiety. The last of his four children had left for college a few months before. Now he and his wife are at home alone and they've discovered that they no longer know each other. This is a common story. They have never been away for a weekend together. All their vacations and activities involved the kids. They didn't even watch TV together. He would watch a program with two of the kids in one room and she in another room with the other two kids. Now they're alone and he doesn't have a clue how to talk with her about anything but practical details. He's feeling very overwhelmed and uncomfortable. As we explored this in more depth, it became clear that his parents never spent time together, just the two of them, sharing thoughts and feelings, holding hands, enjoying each other. This points to part of the problem. Most of us have not had modeled in our families the importance of spending quality time regularly with our mate. As a result, we don't learn the great value and essential need of having time to nourish that relationship. Nor are we shown the many ways of being together. We are handicapped by guilt about all the things we are not doing – taking the kids with us, cleaning the house – and lack of skills.

***

Again nature beckons us. She urges us to put aside the tasks that concern and consume us and come spend time with her to nourish our relationships. Even though thoughts of everyday life may still preoccupy us for a time, we increase the possibility of dropping those concerns if we physically remove ourselves from these distractions. How hard it is to be there for each other when the children want our undivided attention or the house needs cleaning. Nature aids in the transition from the world of secular concerns into the sacred world of the most within. As we move away from the external world of work, children, home and other responsibilities, nature helps us move into the inner world of intimacy with Self and other. Think of this time as a short "vacation." By moving away from the outer world we "vacate" or empty ourselves of all its pulls on us. Thus, we create an opening in our soul into which our beloved can then enter.

Many couples associate being in nature to vacation time. They travel to the Caribbean to wander the endless beaches that border the turquoise sea and to lie in the sand blissfully soaking up the sun. Or, they drive up to the cabin on the lake and spend lazy days floating on an inflatable raft or meandering through the woods. This certainly can be vital and nourishing time to spend together. But we need not wait until we have extended time off to be in nature with our mate. Regardless of where we live, we can find some nature place nearby, even if it is only a small park on a city street corner. While there may still be distractions here, they are not the same as the distractions at home that draw us into activity and away from each other, but can, in fact, draw us to each other and become "grist for the mill" of our relationship.

Oftentimes we have a number of nature places available to us and when both people enjoy the same kind of place then the choice of where to go is easy. But what about when she likes to wander along the beach in the late afternoon sun gathering beach stones and he likes to meander down the river paddling a canoe? If we are to move into the very within place of our relationship then we must enter into the world of the other. If he feels most relaxed, centered and powerful at the helm of a small sailboat tacking across the lake, then it is essential, if she is to know him fully, for her to share that experience. If she feels most energized, sensual and connected to her real Self wandering through open meadows, he will not know these deep parts of her unless he comes into her world. Conscious intention is needed on both sides. He must offer the invitation into his nature place and she must accept. This mutual willingness to enter the other's world, to observe the unfolding of Self and other in that world, is an entrance into the deep within of relationship.

Intimacy can also be enhanced when we find a nature spot that becomes "our place." As we revisit that place over time, we develop a relationship with it. The place becomes familiar and we become more and more at ease in this familiarity. When our intention is to be there with our lover, to open ourselves to each other and the needs of our relationship, then this intention accompanies us as we enter our place and we can feel our consciousness shift to a deeper level. The external world recedes and we can enter the inner world of Self and other.

⁂

Clare and David have been in a mutually neglectful relationship for almost 15 years. Each of them has suffered from an early lack of "good enough" parenting that has left them mostly unable to nurture themselves and each other. Clare has been in therapy with me for some time and this has been helpful to their relationship. A couple of years ago, she had an intuition to buy a sailboat. She and David had gone sailing together early on, but raising their two kids had put a halt to that. Now that the kids are older, Clare went ahead and bought the boat. They go sailing every weekend. This has helped their relationship significantly. Being away from home is important since that represents the scene of conflict and emotional abuse. Being on the water seems to help, too, perhaps because of the deep unconscious connection we have to water as mother, water as womb. Here Clare and David can get a kind of mothering that they did not get in childhood. They are carried and gently rocked by this powerful and nurturing mother. For men, especially, sailing seems to allow mothering to happen in an acceptable, but usually unconscious, way. Being on the water together quiets down their conflicts, renews their energy and engages them in working cooperatively. They share simple meals and periods of silence. While this nature setting would increase the conflicts for another couple, Clare and David have found just the right nature place in which to nurture their relationship.

## Jeanne

Ted and Sue are going through an extraordinarily difficult time in their relationship. A second marriage for both of them, they have been together for about twelve years. While they have been having difficulties for some time, the very fabric of their relationship has been threatened since Sue found out that Ted was involved with another woman. On top of this, his company is downsizing and he is about to lose his job. Polarized by the deep pain, anger and guilt of all that is happening, they have been unable to talk. Sue gets enraged and Ted shuts down completely. At my suggestion, they began taking walks together along a lakeside path near their home. At first, they would go there and just yell at each other or cry. But slowly, over time, they have begun to talk more deeply, to explore whether their relationship can continue. While they have not, as yet, made a decision about this, now when the silence between them is frozen, one or the other suggests a walk along the lake. Something opens up for them and they can express their deeper feelings. And while this is no guarantee that their mutual wounds can be healed enough to mend the relationship, the time they take to be together in nature is moving them into the "most within" of themselves, each other and their relationship.

While both of these relationships are on the "difficult" end of the continuum, time spent in nature has helped to shift something. While it has not worked miracles, it has helped one couple, who have no intention of ending their relationship, to find a space in which they are able to nurture each other, and the other couple to move more deeply and honestly into their pain and conflict, seeking resolution and healing. Intimacy, after all, does not mean sharing only what feels good, but also entering into the darkness that is present in each of us.

Just as we have talked about being present to nature and to our own deeper Self in nature through connection to our senses, the same lessons hold true for being present to our mate. Make every effort to leave the mundane world behind. This means no cameras, no watches, no binoculars, no beepers, no cell phones! All of these distract us from nature and each other. First, it is necessary to allow ourselves to become present in nature. Take the time to feel the breeze on your skin, touch the rough bark of the trees or feel your feet in the warm sand. Reach out and touch a leaf or pick up a stone or a sea shell. Smell the air, listen to the sounds around you. You may begin to feel your body relaxing. Perhaps the concerns of everyday life are beginning to drop away. As your body relaxes, you begin to re-enter it. We are so often detached from our body and its sensations. It is not necessary to talk with your mate during this time, just allow space for becoming present. Listen again to the sounds around you. Perhaps a chipmunk scampers in the dry leaves alongside the path. Or waves crash against the rocks beneath your feet. Notice the colors, all the different shades of blue, green, yellow, red. Take in the array of colors of the sky or the flowers as you breathe in. You may be becoming more aware of your body now. Nature is sensuous, erotic and alive. Diane Ackerman describes the scent of a flower, for instance, as declaring "to all the world that it is fertile, available, and desirable...Its smell reminds us in vestigial ways of fertility, vigor, life-force, all the optimism, expectancy, and passionate bloom of youth. We inhale its ardent aroma and, no matter what our ages, we feel young and nubile in a world aflame with desire."[16] As you let in all the sensations of nature, your body will begin to feel more alive.

When you and your mate are together in nature in this way, with the intention of being present to each other and allowing the unfolding of the most within, the sensuous connection you have made with nature may draw you to your lover in the same way. As you become more connected to your senses, you are becoming more alive and the desire to make contact with your mate is stirred up. You may find yourself reaching to hold her hand or watching as the wind plays gently with her hair. You may reach out to rest your hand on his back or touch the highlights in his hair you never noticed before. You may find yourselves playfully bumping up against each other as you walk. While our own mothers and father may have been frightened or threatened by our physicality and sensuality, Mother Nature delights in the sensual and

the erotic. She displays her own sensuality flamboyantly in the vibrant colors of the meadow grasses and wildflowers; in the silky texture of a gently swaying fern; in the sight of the voluptuous magnolia blossoms; in the luscious taste of just picked blackberries; in the musky, wet smell of the earth after a spring rain.

Time spent together in nature can awaken all the slumbering part of Self: the sensuous and sexual self, the deeper thinking, philosophical self; the spiritual self, the playful self. Opportunity, combined with nature's invitation to go deeper, can stir thoughtful conversation, fantasies, dreams, moments of communion, moments of play that would not otherwise happen with the demands of everyday life. Each of these experiences can help us to connect to the most within parts of our mate.

<hr/>

## 🌸 Bill

Maureen, a woman in her forties, came to a recent workshop of ours on the healing qualities of nature. A week or so afterwards, she told me that she and her husband had gone back the following day to the place where we gave the workshop. As they walked through the woods and meadows and down along the water's edge, they began to speak deeply about their life philosophies, particularly their differing philosophies on raising children. They had been unable to talk of this at other times and their differences were causing problems with their daughter and getting in the way of their relationship. Taking this time in nature for just the two of them helped them to come to a greater clarity on the issue. "It's remarkable," Maureen told me, "that you can live with someone for so many years and not really know them." But after this walk, she and her husband felt that they knew each other a little more.

Being in nature together can also help us to see ourselves more clearly in our relationships. Without the distractions of the mundane world, we are more apt to notice who or how we are with others. In our most recent couples workshop, when Dana and Kenny came back from their walk, Dana described how "I suddenly realized that I was walking far ahead of Kenny, telling him which way we should go and where we should put down the blanket!" From the work she has done in therapy, Dana is aware of her tendency to be the "take charge" one in their relationship. But, seeing herself play out that role so clearly in their walk – and seeing Kenny's role as follower – brought her to a deeper level of "knowing" their style of relating.

### 🌸 Jeanne

For Bill and me, walking through the woods or along the river stirs us to share our deepest thoughts, troubles or creative ideas. Without the distractions of home and work, I feel deeply listened to and am able to listen deeply. When we walk together to the waterfall, I am awakened to my own deep feminine. This part of me is expressed in different images each time I am there. After we sit for a while in silent meditation, I share with Bill my inner images of an abundant mother, spilling over, laughing joyously, thunderously, filling me. In this quiet space, opening to a rich part of my Self allows me to share that most within with Bill.

Another day, down at the river's edge, we sit again in silent meditation and "listen to what the river says." Bill, in his Taurus nature, has been stuck in the mud for a while. Inviting me into his most within, he shares with me that it's time for him to let go of a recent conflict and move on, move back into the flow of life. As we walk the dirt path alongside the river, we watch the changing colors of the water: here it is dark blue, here it is brown; here it reflects the ever-green of the surrounding trees. We stop to follow the motion

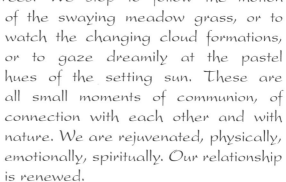

of the swaying meadow grass, or to watch the changing cloud formations, or to gaze dreamily at the pastel hues of the setting sun. These are all small moments of communion, of connection with each other and with nature. We are rejuvenated, physically, emotionally, spiritually. Our relationship is renewed.

Another way of being present to the deeper Self of our mate is by encouraging the other to listen to the urging of the "soul voice" within and to the beckoning of nature. If we think of the word *encourage* as *putting courage in*, then our words of encouragement to our beloved can give him or her the courage to follow a spontaneous urge to roll down a bluff, lean down and smell a flower, run down a hill, have a snowball fight, climb a tree or go skinny dipping. Often we ignore these impulses because they feel silly, childish or stupid. These thoughts block the desire – the child self and the adult self are in conflict – and we don't act, missing a moment of delightful playfulness, immense freedom or deep connection to our Self, our mate and nature. These parts of Self were so often lost or neglected in childhood and now need encouragement to come out into the world. Here's a simple example. Last summer, Bill and I were walking across the backyard toward the house when I got this sudden urge to play leap frog like we did when we were kids. But at the same time I felt silly, childlike and vulnerable. After all, what if I say I want to play leap frog and Bill looks at me like I'm crazy – we're too old to play that! But I risk it and he laughs and says, "Let's do it!" and gets down on all fours. In a few moments we are tumbling around on the grass, laughing until we have tears in our eyes! Another time, we were walking in the woods in the snow and Bill stopped when we came to a hill. "I really feel like rolling down this hill," he said hesitantly. "Go for it!" I said and followed right behind him. We landed at the bottom entangled with each other, again laughing at our pure silliness. These are small moments that we recall with a smile, that wouldn't have happened without the openness and encouragement of the other.

When we are with our mate in nature, often the urges that we feel are these childlike urges to be playful. When I talk with people about a time when they were connected with nature, invariably they tell me stories from childhood. It is, after all, our child self that has been so deeply wounded and fears coming out into the world, expecting to be wounded again. With the encouragement of our "playmate," the child self is safe and free to climb on the rocks, roll down a hill, sing in the woods at the top of his voice or dance in a meadow. Without criticism, without judgments, early wounds begin to heal, we feel safer in allowing the other into the most within, and our relationship with our Self and our mate deepens.

The desire for intimacy is not limited to our mate relationships. Most of us would love to feel a deeper connection to our children, friends, parents and others. Children love, more than any other place, to be outside. They care little if it is too hot or too cold or rainy or snowy. This is their territory. The more weather the better! To be there with them, at least for intermittent spaces of time, can open opportunities for all kinds of talks about life, beauty, God, sexuality and a host of other subjects that are so very important. But we rarely get to hear what they have to say or get a chance to share our own thoughts and feelings with them.

Walking down Main Street the other day, we overheard the following conversation between a mother and her four-year-old daughter:

"Come on, honey, we're holding people up. Town is not the best place to collect rocks," mom says as her little girl stoops to pick up pebbles from the sidewalk.

93

"Where can we collect rocks, mommy?" the little girl asks.

"Oh, there are lots of places I can take you to collect rocks."

"And then we can have a  nice walk together!" her daughter says with assurance.

This is a simple but telling conversation. The little girl knows that in town they are hurried. Mommy has places to go and things to purchase. But in nature, someplace where she can collect rocks, she and mommy can be together, unhurried, explore together, find things and "have a nice walk together." She makes the invitation, hopefully mommy responds.

Jane Goodall, famous for her work with gorillas, tells a lovely story of how her "remarkable and understanding mother" early on fostered her love of nature and all creatures and taught her at the same time about the nature of things:

> Once she found me watching in fascination the movements of a handful of earthworms I had taken up to my bed. Instead of expressing horror and demanding I throw them out, she quietly told me they would be dead if they could not get back to the Earth. I ran with them into the garden.[17]

Instead of being upset about the worms in her daughter's bed, Goodall's mother was sensitive to the importance of the bond between child and nature. Surely her wisdom enriched their relationship. Anita Barrows, a poet and child psychologist, tells a story of her daughter's early bond with nature and her own experience of this with her:

When my daughter Viva was small enough to be carried in a backpack, I used to walk with her almost daily in the open hills of Tilden Park, on the east side of San Francisco Bay. It struck me one day that her babbling hushed to a whisper as we entered a grove of Monterey pine. Under the spun light of pine needles, in the cool summer afternoon, I, too, felt hushed, but Viva's response seemed to me to be entirely her own, and I noticed it many times thereafter, as though something in her resonated instinctually with the changed air, the canopy of branches, the mysterious flickering of shadow.[18]

A shared, deeply-felt moment between mother and daughter, even at such a young age, is a moment of profound intimacy. Both are present to nature; mother is present to daughter. This lays a foundation for a relationship of ongoing intimate moments and a sharing, each with the other, of the most within.

We do not need to interact with our children in nature in order to enter into their world. Sometimes, because of their age, they will not allow us in as a participant and all we can do, to be respectful, is observe. One of the most memorable times with my two sons was just this kind of time. We had gone to Vermont for a week. They were twelve and thirteen and had brought along a friend about the same age. Because of their ages and the fact that they are boys, they were only interested in my very limited participation in their activities. At the same time, they needed me to get them to the places they wanted to go. So I was given entrance, through circumstance, to their decidedly male world.

No matter where we went, Chris, John and their friend, Tim were totally engaged with their surroundings. In the course of that week, I watched them become fishermen, fishing for hours along the rocky outcroppings of the lake; hunters, returning home to slaughter (literally) their catch, examining in the process, fish guts and the workings of fish jaws. They were warriors on a quest to conquer the highest mountain or jump from the highest rock ledge into the river below. I was a woman among these boy-men and aware, more profoundly then I had ever been, of the differences between us. I longed for the company of my own tribe, to be in a place that was familiar. And yet, I felt honored to be privy to the workings of the male tribe in a way I had not been before. Much of the time my heart was in my throat as I watched them climb heights and approach edges. But in observing them, I learned that they are not foolish; they take risks but with caution and respect for their surroundings.

We went to an air show near the end of our trip. Men flying their man-made machines into the heavens. Before this I would have pooh-poohed the whole idea of men's need to build a machine and take off into the sky. But, now, I saw it all differently. In some strange, unspeakable way, I understood. Observing Chris and John and Tim in their interactions with nature over these several days, I suddenly understood this way of being in nature too. It has to do with challenge and risk taking, pushing against edges; and profound trust.

When the glider was released from the plane, I thought is was magnificent, floating high up on the wind. I thought how absolutely trusting one must be to let oneself be guided totally by the whims of Zephyrus; the courage it takes to give oneself over in that way. And I was in awe.

Spending time in this way, my kids and I gave each other some important and beautiful things. I gave them the opportunity to have some adventures, silently giving them the space and freedom to stretch their wings and test themselves. They, in turn, allowed me into their world, to see them in ways I had not seen them before. I felt I knew these boy-men more deeply then and appreciated more their intrinsic natures.

## 🌸 Bill

While my son, Mark, was a student at Brandeis University in Massachusetts, he discovered Walden Pond. He would go there often with friends to walk or swim across the pond. Over time, it also became a place of solitude for him; a place to be with his own thoughts and emotional struggles. Knowing my love of nature and deep regard for Thoreau's philosophy, Mark invited me to walk with him at Walden Pond on one of my weekend visits. I shared his enthusiasm for the place. Spontaneously, a younger Mark (in his 6'7" frame!) appeared, skipping stones across the surface of the pond and challenging me to try and outdo him. Of course, he won, but not by much! We laughed, reminisced about other father-son competitions and talked philosophically about life. On subsequent visits, we were invariably drawn to spend some time at Walden. We both knew that at some point in our sojourn there the talk would shift into a deeper place. We would talk about our relationship, about finding our own way to be a man in this world, about relationships with women . . . Walden became a place where, as father and son, we could share our most within. I like to think that Thoreau's spirit smiled as he witnessed us sauntering through his beloved woods and along the edge of his pond, responding to its legacy as a place of deep connectedness.

I often share my love of nature with patients, too, and am profoundly touched by the many ways in which it deepens our relationship. One of my favorite stories is about a young boy, David, 11-years old. He was curious about a pen and ink drawing in my office of a wolf and a crow. I told him stories about my long-standing relationship with crows, about how smart they are, how community minded they are, how they wait for the leftover food that I put out for them each day, but most of all how playful crows are. David was intrigued by my stories. Oftentimes during our sessions, we would make paper airplanes while we talked. He had become proficient at this after spending many hours locked in his room by his angry stepfather. The week after my crow stories, David came back to me with a story of his own:

When I went home last week, Doc, I was out in the backyard flying my plane. I noticed a crow sitting up in a tree watching me. So I watched him, too. I kept scaling my plane for a while and then one time I threw it and the crow flew down and snatched the plane in its beak! He flew up about twenty or thirty feet, dropped the plane, flew down below it and caught it again! Then he took the plane and dropped it on the roof of the garage, landed there himself and started cawing at me.

David was surprised to have his own experience of the crow's playfulness. He also liked sharing it with me and knowing something his friends didn't know. We had a good laugh together. In traditional psychotherapy this kind of self-disclosure might be frowned upon. But sharing my crow experiences with him allowed for an opening in our relationship and deepened my bond with David.

⁂

"I only went out for a walk and finally concluded to stay out until sundown, for going out, I found was really going in."[19] So wrote John Muir in the late 1800s. His walks in nature were solitary, as it seems to be with most of the early nature writers we have encountered. Certainly in solitude outside we "go in." But, with attention and intention, whether with our mate, child, friend or some other beloved, when we go out into nature together, we can also go into the most within.

# SIMPLICITY

 **Jeanne**

    I am sitting at the edge of a grassy field finishing my morning meditation. As my attention shifts from the inner world to the outer, I become aware of the songs of the birds in the background, the sound of the crickets in the foreground and the distant droning of a tractor mower. As I open my eyes and look around, I whisper, "Wow!" There isn't much here: newly mown grass, sweet-musky smells, a border of trees around the edge of the field, a passing butterfly, blue sky dotted with wispy clouds, the warmth of the sun . . . but still I whisper, "Wow!" At this moment I would like to stay here forever. The beauty and simplicity of what surrounds me sinks into my belly. Though I am struggling with a deep sadness inside, at this moment, in this place, life feels very simple. I need not do anything. I need not rid myself of the sadness. I need only be, just as I am at this very moment.

    The dew is still on the ground and silken threads weave themselves, criss-crossing from one strand of grass to another. Barely visible, I can see them only when I cock by head a certain way and the sun glistens off of them. I wonder, who is the weaver of this light-reflecting tapestry? Diagonally across from me, way at the top of a long-dead tree, sits an osprey. Is she resting from a morning flight? Surveying the landscape for a meal? Whatever, she is still and silent and helps me to remember that same place in myself. The air is cool, the sun is warm. A breeze blows from the other side of the field. I can see and hear it as it brushes past the trees, rustling the leaves. A bee alights on my writing pad. My first impulse is to stiffen but I quickly remember what I have learned about how to "be" with bees. I am still and quiet and say, "Hello in there!" I think, perhaps, he wants me to write about him, too. A big, fuzzy, black caterpillar with bright orange bands around her middle crawls through the grass onto my blanket. When I move she stops and tucks her head in hoping, I suppose, that I cannot see her. When she moves again I use my yellow lined paper to guide her off the blanket. She climbs on and I deposit her in the grass to continue on her journey. I look up and see a butterfly before me and another osprey flying overhead in the distance. My first osprey friend still sits in the tree branch. Just sitting. In the midst of all this activity going on around me I, too, am just sitting. My sadness has not left me but I am at peace in this surrounding stillness and simplicity.

<hr/>

While I observe nature as a model of simplicity, in truth, nature is extraordinarily complex. The complexity lies in the interdependence of species; the unending processes of symbiosis, mutuality and cooperation; the essential relationships between predators and prey. When looked at as a whole, these underlying processes, constantly growing and changing, living and dying, are intricate. But, the expression of this complexity and intricacy is in a simplicity of behavior that comes, perhaps, from living from instinct without the burden of "mind" as we experience it. I speculate about this, of course, from my observations, but cannot really know the true nature of, let's say, a tree or a turtle. From all appearances, it seems that a tree does not struggle to know its true nature. It just is treeness. A turtle or a fox does not question what it means to be "turtle" or "fox" but just is turtleness or foxness. I, on the other hand, am continually pondering, questioning, considering, exploring what it means to be "Jeanne" and how my Jeanne-ness is expressed in the world. My mind, with all its wanderings and wonderings, seems often to get in the way of the full and spontaneous expression of my true nature. Not to mention the influences of all the other "creatures" different from myself who have had a part in raising me. Am I the same as them? Am I to be like them? Or am I different from them? What if they had encouraged my different-ness from them, my own unique characteristics, instead of expecting me to be just like them? Would my struggle to be "just only Jeanne" be less?

When I am outside among the trees and birds and sky, even if I am only lying in my hammock in the backyard, the struggle is less. I fall easily into the hammock, stare mindlessly up through the trees into the blue ocean of sky and a deep sigh issues forth. I feel the tightness in my body relax, a letting go. No pressure here to be "mom" or "mate" or "lover" or "friend" or "therapist" and fill all the expectations that are projected onto these roles by myself and others. Here in my hammock or in the woods or at the river I can be "mindless," less in my mind, more in my body. I can turn my gaze from the external expectations of the world and focus inward, not on mind and its eternal questions, but on just being. Breathing helps me shift my awareness.

But even the simple act of breathing seems to have become complex. The pace at which we move through life affects how we breathe, and the way in which we breathe affects the way in which we move through the world. Most of us breathe incorrectly to begin with, from the lungs rather than the diaphragm. When we breathe from the chest we breathe in short, quick breaths. This puts stress on the lungs and heart and leaves the body in a constant state of feeling stressed. This constant stress can then lead to anxiety. Stress and anxiety, in turn, cause us to take shallow breaths, increasing the anxiety and creating a cycle that is difficult – and simple – to break.

Another aspect of our difficulty breathing is that the air we breathe has become noxious and toxic to our systems. Think of the additional stress to our bodies as our lungs work overtime to filter out all of the toxic "stuff" from the air. This physical stress can easily become emotional stress. Again, each compounds the other. In spite of this, breathing is one of life's simple acts. It does not take thought or mind or any kind of conscious action. We just breathe. It is an act of the autonomic nervous system. But changing the way we breathe so that we are breathing in a relaxed, easy and free way, so that we are taking in the "breath of life," takes conscious action. To begin to breathe in a healthier way, it can be helpful to go to our nature place. Outside and away from car fumes, industrial smoke, the recycled, stale air of tightly sealed offices and other noxious oxygen, we can more easily retrain ourselves to breathe properly. When we are outside, too, our breathing is in direct relationship and cooperation with the plant world. We take in the oxygen that the plants give off and, in turn, supply them with their needed carbon dioxide. Mutuality. Equal exchange. Cooperation. Relationship. Done with awareness, just breathing can be a simple moment of communion with the plant world. This same act of mutual giving and receiving also can occur with the plants and trees we keep in our homes and offices. In fact, if we spend extended periods of time indoors, plants and trees should be an essential part of our inside environment. Whether outside or inside, just a few moments of time given throughout each day to simple, conscious breathing can enhance the quality and capacity of our breathing, re-energize us, reduce stress and anxiety, and as Thich Nhat Hanh would say, help us to connect with the Peace that underlies all things.[20]

Initially, just allow yourself to become aware of your breath. Do not change the way you breathe, just notice your breath. After a few moments, begin to take in deep breaths. Breathe so that the air goes into your lungs and then deeper still, all the way down to the center of your belly. If you can, lie down on the ground or sit with your back against a tree or rock, close your eyes, put your hands on your belly just below your naval and breathe deeply. Feel your belly rise with each breath that you take in, and fall with each breath that you let out. Extending the exhale will help to increase physical relaxation. For as long as you are comfortable, continue with this focused breathing, paying attention to each breath you take in and each breath you let out. Consider, too, the conscious relationship that is developing at that moment between you and your relatives in the plant world.

## Bill

Simplicity also has to do with time and rhythms. Think about this: only humans wear wristwatches. No other creature uses a mechanical device to tell them when to sleep, eat, work or play. They either respond to their own internal clock or to external cues from the natural world, such as the amount of daylight. We, on the other hand, rely on clocks to tell us when to do things. We eat because it is "lunchtime" even though we aren't hungry. We don't sleep when we're tired because it isn't yet "bedtime." Many people become anxious if they don't know what time it is. Years ago, I had a supervisor who was an intriguing mix of psychoanalyst and Buddhist. He shared with me his fantasy to eliminate the numbers on clocks and watches and set them all permanently to read NOW. Then, as the Buddhists suggest, we might all live in the present moment. Perhaps the other creatures are the true Buddhists! If we follow their modeling to "be in the now" we can begin to incorporate that teaching into our daily lives.

I sometimes talk with patients about the natural pacing of different animals as a way of helping them to connect with their own rhythm. We all feel the pressure to keep up with our fast-moving, high-tech world, but I wonder how many of us are moving at a rate of speed that feels true to our nature. Again, we can look to the animal world as a model. Notice all the differences: the painstakingly slow, deliberate movement of the turtle; the lumbering movement of the bear; the frenetic pace of the squirrel; the graceful soaring of the hawk; and the fleet grace of a jaguar in full stride. For each of these creatures, their speed of movement in the world and the rhythmic patterns of their day reflect the essence of their nature. Their way of being in the world expresses their turtleness, bearness, squirrelness, hawkness and jaguarness. What about us? Do we move about in our world at a pace and in a rhythm that suits our nature?

I am reminded of Anthony, an executive in the financial department of a major corporation. He is good at his job but he hates it. He knows that the job alienates him from his basic nature, yet he has been doing it for so long that he has lost touch with who he is. During one of our sessions, we did some guided imagery to help Anthony reconnect with his deeper Self. After some relaxational breathing I led him through the following imagery:

> Imagine yourself walking in some nature setting, some place that you feel most comfortable, most alive, most "at home". Walk along by yourself noticing what is around you and paying attention to how it feels to be in this place. After a while you come to a circular clearing with a fire in the center and two rocks on either side as sitting places. Sit down on one of the rocks. Across the clearing comes a Wise Old Man. Trust whatever image of a Wise Old Man comes into your mind. This old

man knows you very well and knows exactly what you need. Notice how it feels to be in his presence. After a while the Wise Man gives you something that symbolizes your true Self. Just trust whatever happens, knowing that he is there to help and guide you.

After a while, I asked Anthony to share with me what was happening and what he saw. He said that he saw this image of a creature, "half butterfly, half dragonfly." He intuitively liked the image although its meaning was not immediately obvious. When Anthony opened his eyes, we discussed what thoughts he had about the half butterfly, half dragonfly. He talked about the butterfly as so colorful and so free to fly wherever it wants. This, in contrast to the drabness of his work and how confining it is for him.

"I love to paint. I love the richness of the colors and how alive I feel when I am painting. How that contrasts with how I feel at work!"

Anthony then thought for a while about the dragonfly part of the image. The aspect that most struck him was its tendency to hover over a spot for a long time.

"I am a reflective thinker, I like to ponder things for a while and think deeply about important issues. What I can't stand about the corporate world is how it so highly values quick thinking and fast, often shallow, answers."

The image was helping him to connect with these aspects of Anthonyness that he had to suppress each day. Clearly the pacing of the corporate world does not support or encourage Anthony's natural rhythm or important aspects of his essential nature. Without greater expression of the butterfly-dragonfly part of himself, Anthony's life is seriously out of balance.

Like Anthony, most of our lives are out of balance. So much time spent on the outer life and so little on the inner life; so much time at work and so little at play; so much time with clients and customers and so little with mates, children and friends; so much time living and working inside boxes and so little time outside with the other creatures . . . All of this produces physiological, psychological and spiritual disequilibrium. Most of us need to find a new balance. Balance is not static, but a moving back and forth, in and out of, to and fro'. Observing the natural world and its ways, we can see the dynamic movement as a basic law: night and day, winter and summer, work and play, activity and dormancy.

## 🐚 Jeanne

A couple of years ago, Bill and I spent ten lovely, relaxing days on a small island of rainforest in the West Indies called Dominica. The name means "Sunday," which we loved, since Sundays for us are truly a day of rest and renewal. So there we were with ten days of Sundays all to ourselves! We did some hiking and touring around the island, but most of our time was spent resting, wandering through the magnificent gardens of the small wilderness retreat where we stayed, talking and sharing time together, soaking in hot mineral springs, and eating good food. It took me about half a day to adapt to this slowed-down pace. By the time we had to leave, I felt so connected to my natural rhythms, so fully in my body, so rested and quieted down, I knew I wanted to feel this way forever.

Returning home, all the undone tasks I had left behind begged for completion. Children, work, home and finances all needed my attention. I could easily slip into the frenetic pace of life in New York. I felt sad, as though I had lost something. The time in Dominica stirred in me a longing for a simpler life. It is a spiritual longing as I experience it. A desire to go directly to the Source, unencumbered, to carry only what is essential for the journey, to have no distractions and no attachments. Buddha, Jesus, Lao Tzu and other spiritual teachers have tried to guide us about the importance of attuning ourselves to this yearning and have modeled ways of responding to its call. The essence of their teachings is to recognize that we have an inner spiritual need for simplicity and when our external world mirrors that, the inner state is easier to attain. Our culture, with its obsession for technology and materialism, responds to this inner urging in the opposite way. Striving for simplicity we purchase all kinds of devices guaranteed to make our lives "simpler." We purchase ever-increasing numbers of these "helpful" tools. And, yet, people still complain that life is too complicated and they don't have time to do the things they love to do or be with the people they love. It is a paradox. We are seeking simplicity and yet the very objects that are supposed to help us attain this have made our lives even busier. Perhaps it is because, while we think that more material things will make our lives simpler, we have to work more to make the money that is necessary to buy these objects of our desire. And while they may sometimes free up time, we spend that time with the object, or tool, or machine and all that it enables us to do. We are constantly doing rather than just being. There is no longer time for musing and mulling, for long, leisurely walks in the woods with our child, for heartfelt talks with a friend, for quiet meditation on the beach, for developing our own personal relationship with God. Our attempts to simplify are in direct opposition to this inner yearning.

Bill and I returned from Dominica with a deeper commitment to find simplicity and balance in our lives. For Bill, that has meant following the advice of Thich Nhat Hanh and spending a morning each week in mindfulness, walking, contemplating and meditating in the woods.[21] For me, it has meant continually struggling to attend, moment to moment, to my own needs and rhythms. Resting when I need rest, eating when I am hungry, making space for myself - having, as Virginia Woolf would say, "a room of my own"[22] - balancing work and play, solitude and relationship. Each of us needs to find our own way, suited to our nature, that responds to this yearning for simplicity.

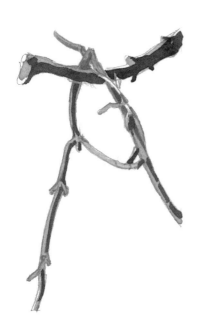

# SELF-FORGIVENESS

## ✿ Bill

While I was going through my divorce, I was so wracked with guilt that I would imagine myself each morning strapping a pack onto my back. The pack, I imagined, was filled with stones of all sizes that represented my burden of guilt. Some of the stones were the guilt I felt at breaking up my family; some were the guilt of leaving my two sons; others were guilt for wanting a different kind of relationship with a woman and now having that. Those were the largest and heaviest stones in my pack. Other, smaller stones symbolized so many of the things that I had felt guilt for over my lifetime, all come rushing back to add to my already overwhelming burden.

But, that's often how it is with guilt. When we feel guilty about one thing, in creeps all the old guilt. And we all carry a pack on our backs, too, though we may not even be aware of it. At least I've yet to meet someone who doesn't. The stones we each carry can represent many kinds of guilt; for the hurt and harm we have caused others; for our failures; for our deeds of action or inaction; for our betrayals of Self. Some of the guilt we carry is healthy guilt that results from a fully formed conscience and allows us to recognize when we have done wrong, make amends, forgive ourselves and then move on. These stones are fairly easily removed from our pack. Unhealthy guilt, on the other hand, is out of proportion to the offense, weighs us down for long periods of time without resolution, is not relieved through making amends and is more connected to our core feelings about ourselves

117

than to what we have actually done. Forgiveness, in this case, seems impossible.[23]

Even more insidious is when we are not even conscious that we are feeling guilty. Instead we act in ways that are self-destructive and reveal a deep feeling of personal unworthiness.

For instance, Ann, a woman in her mid-sixties, had been married for many years to a man who was physically and emotionally abusive with her and her daughter. She only divorced him when her daughter was grown and out of the house and now sees so clearly the devastating effects his abuse had on her. Since the divorce, Ann has felt her life is really over. She rarely socializes and has had no other relationships with men. Only recently has she become aware of the tremendous burden of guilt she has been carrying for not divorcing this abusive man sooner. This unconscious guilt was responsible for her feelings of unworthiness, that nothing good could happen in her life.

Anyone who has ever suffered with unhealthy or unconscious guilt knows what I am describing. If we continue to carry our pack of "guilt-stones" unexamined, we become so weighted down that life becomes joyless, we become fearful, and we are unable to act in our own behalf. Psychological and spiritual growth can come to a grinding halt unless we begin to examine and heal our burden of guilt.

---

Oftentimes we have no way of seeking forgiveness from the ones we have wounded. They may have died or be unwilling to forgive. Sometimes we have betrayed someone and they are not even aware of our betrayal. We suffer the guilt of knowing what we have done and want to tell the other in order to relieve our own conscience. But this may not be in their best interests. What do we do then? We may quietly make amends in some way, but after a while realize that we still carry significant guilt. Sometimes there is no possible external source of forgiveness; it is ourselves we have wounded. Who do we turn to for forgiveness when we have betrayed our deeper Self through neglect, addictions, attachment to destructive relationships or unrealistic expectations of ourselves? Most people might say, "Well, God forgives me." But in our experience, even when someone feels forgiven by God, they often are still unable to forgive themselves. How frequently we hear people say, "I know God has forgiven me, the problem is that I can't forgive myself." Certainly rituals of reconciliation are helpful, and to feel forgiveness from God or a Higher Power can help to lessen the burden of guilt. But unless we can also turn toward an inner source of forgiveness we will never be fully unburdened. We need to do the inner work of forgiveness and then we can be even more receptive to the forgiveness that is possible from outer sources.

Most people, we find, don't even think of forgiving themselves. Even though they say, "The problem is I can't forgive myself," they don't even really believe that self-forgiveness is possible. We can forgive others or be forgiven by others, but we have so much trouble forgiving ourselves. In struggling to understand the reasons for this we have found that religious and family experiences play a large role in how we approach forgiveness. To begin with, in traditional religions we are taught that forgiveness comes from an outside source. We learn to forgive others and to seek forgiveness from others or from God, but we rarely hear about forgiving self. This is changing somewhat as more people explore other avenues of spirituality such as twelve-step programs or the Course in Miracles. However, the primary emphasis still seems to be on forgiving others, making amends and seeking forgiveness from others. The importance of self-forgiveness is still minimized.

But we can work from this idea of seeking forgiveness from someone, God, a Higher Power, to learn how to experience forgiveness from the inside. In each of the major religions there is a mystical aspect that teaches about "God within us." In the Gnostic gospel of Thomas, Jesus explains this God within to his disciples. He tells them that the kingdom of God is not a place, but a consciousness that exists within us and beyond us and that, in order to realize the kingdom we must have self-knowledge. "Rather, the kingdom is inside of you, and it is outside of you," Jesus said.[24] This inner connection to the divine, then, is a source for us to call upon in our struggle to forgive ourselves. Knowing that there is something within us that is greater than our everyday self can help us connect to a wellspring of compassionate understanding. However, most of us have not been taught about this God within or we were not taught ways of connecting to this inner divine. We were more typically exposed to the concept of an external God who offers forgiveness when we seek it through prayer or religious ritual.

⁂

Frequently, our families fostered the religious belief that we must be forgiving of others. "Don't blame your brother," a child is told, "he didn't mean it." At the same time, within our families, we were shamed and made to feel unforgivable. "How could you be so mean. You're a

120

bad girl!" Sometimes parents are embarrassed by the things their children do or say and, instead of accepting their naturally childish behaviors, or helping the child find a way to make amends or say "I'm sorry" for mistakes, all too frequently the child is told "Sorry isn't enough," or "It's too late to say you're sorry. You should've thought about that sooner!" The words "I'm sorry" then lose their power to make amends and the child receives a double message: I must forgive someone for hurting me, but I am not worthy of forgiveness, or it's too late for me to be forgiven. As children, we identify closely with our parents and the things they say to us are replayed constantly in our minds. If no one has ever said, "Forgive yourself," or "Be gentle with yourself," or "We all make mistakes," then we have no internal voice of self-forgiveness. We develop early emotional blocks that carry into adulthood and make forgiving ourselves very difficult.

Some people, we find, have no experience in the process of reconciliation. They come from families where there was little or no overt fighting; conflicts and anger were suppressed. They have no experience in openly hurting or being hurt by another and genuinely healing that hurt by making amends or saying a heartfelt "I'm sorry." For them the whole territory of forgiveness is unfamiliar. In other families, "I'm sorry" is meaningless. For example, when a parent is verbally or physically abusive and apologizes, but then abuses again, the child is expected to forgive the parent, and in fact wants to forgive, but the abuse continues. What do the words "I'm sorry" really mean then? What kinds of messages about forgiveness are being internalized?

In families where children witness frequent conflict, rather than modeling forgiveness, parents actively harbor grudges and hatred. We all know families like this. Uncle Bob isn't invited to family gatherings because of something (no one remembers what) he did 11 years ago. Or, Mom and Dad won't speak for days or weeks or months after an argument. In these families forgiveness is unknown. The "silent treatment" may go on indefinitely or it may just gradually end, but the feelings of anger and resentment remain buried deep within to be used as weapons against the other at another time.

People who are always putting the needs of others first generally find the notion of self-forgiveness selfish, narcissistic or grandiose. It's okay to take care of an emotionally frail parent or an alcoholic spouse, or to devote time and energy to anyone else who may need it, but to take care of oneself by learning how to forgive oneself is not okay. And often these are the people who need self-forgiveness most. They have extremely high expectations of themselves about what they should and shouldn't do and can rarely live up to these unreasonable demands. As a result, they carry a heavy burden of unhealthy guilt.

Finally, self-forgiveness is related to self-image and self-acceptance. This is why it is so much easier to forgive others. We're much more comfortable thinking that someone else is capable of wounding another then to have to admit that about ourselves. For if we are truly to forgive ourselves, then we must look deeply into ourselves at the harm we have caused another. We must look at cherished, but false, self-images and accept the part of us that has the capacity to cause harm. Ultimately, to forgive ourselves means to accept our limitations and our full humanness.

❦

From our psychotherapeutic work and our personal experiences, we have learned that self-forgiveness is a process that happens over time in recognizable stages. Awareness is an initial entrance into this process. This means not only admitting that we have caused harm to another or ourselves, but gaining knowledge and understanding of the notion of self-forgiveness. Part of the purpose of this work is to increase awareness of both the possibility and the essential need in each of us for self-forgiveness. So the first phase in this process, as we have just explored, is awareness.

The second phase is preparation. Forgiveness is deeply mysterious. Only a fool would say, "I know exactly what forgiveness is, where it comes from and how to make it happen." Hopefully we are not fools! And yet, forgiveness does not occur until we prepare ourselves. Perhaps the metaphor of the gardener will help to explain what we mean by preparation.

The experienced gardener knows when he has a good seed that will grow a healthy plant. Yet he does not simply walk over to the field and plant the seed. He knows that the field must be prepared to receive the seed. The ground is covered with weeds and debris; the soil is depleted of nutrients. First the gardener pulls out the weeds, hauls away the debris, turns over the soil and then puts down good fertilizer. After all of this preparation, the soil is ready to receive the seed. The gardener plants it, nurtures it, weeding and watering, until the seed grows into a healthy plant ready for harvesting. Likewise, we are the gardeners who need to prepare the field of our psyches to receive the seed of self-forgiveness.

Our conscious efforts help to make self-forgiveness possible, but when and how it occurs is mysterious and not within our control. This is the passive part. By our active preparation through meditation, imagery, prayer and time in nature we create a mode of receptive openness and then - we wait. Self-forgiveness has its own timetable and cannot be hurried. It does not happen in linear or chronological time, so we cannot say that in three months you will feel forgiven. It occurs in the time of the heart and soul, what the ancient Greeks called "kairos." In that psychospiritual mode of experiencing time, a week can feel like several lifetimes or hours can feel like a few moments. In the work of self forgiving, our conscious mind needs to be patient with the timetable of the heart and soul.

⚜

It is in the preparation phase of self-forgiveness that nature can play such an important catalytic role. When we are seeking forgiveness, we need a place to go to alone where we will feel safe and not self-conscious about what happens. Nature offers herself as a sanctuary, a place of safety and sacredness, where we can do our visualizations, meditations, prayers and self-talking. We need to follow, moment to moment, the healing process of the Self. Our soul knows what we need to heal and anything can happen. We might suddenly start sobbing or fall to our knees or start chanting or talking out loud or singing. We must be able to let that unfold from moment to moment. The freedom just to allow that to occur is almost impossible if there are other people around. Even the presence of the most wonderfully warm and supportive person is inhibiting. We will wonder, "What does he really think of me? How will she react if I just start crying?" Or we will think of the needs of the other or start talking about mundane things. Other parts of the forgiveness journey require a companion or guide. The time in nature should be solitary time. Our companion – nature – is already present.

It is important to designate some particular place in nature for our forgiveness work. When we return again and again to the same place, we may begin to feel, as we approach this place, a quieting down that happens with little or no effort now. A particular place becomes imbued with the power of our forgiveness work, there is a sense of peacefulness, a quieting down of our inner "stuff," a sense of belonging, a rightness about this place. The soul knows why we are here. An inner preparation is happening. It is as if the place beckons us. If we trust deeply, we will feel led to, drawn to, invited to a particular spot. Jeanne, for example, is drawn to the moving water of a stream or brook when she needs self-forgiveness. Combined with the strong pull she feels in general to be near the water, this creates an atmosphere of numinous power just suited to her unique process of self-forgiveness. Bill, on the other hand, is drawn to his grove of pine trees as he has described before. It is there that he experiences the mysterious powers of compassion and forgiveness.

 **Bill**

Theresa, a patient whose mother died shortly after moving to a nursing home, suffered tremendous guilt after her death. Her relationship with her mother had always been filled with ambivalence. As a child, her mother was incessantly critical and Theresa never felt like a "good enough" daughter. As an adult, her criticism continued and Theresa suffered additional doubts about herself as a wife and mother.

As Theresa's mother aged, she became even more difficult to be with. Her husband had been dead for many years and she was estranged from Theresa's sister, who had grown weary of her constant nagging. As her health began to decline, Theresa was the one to care for her. After a time it became clear that her mother could no longer live on her own and that she expected to move in with Theresa. Feeling tremendously guilty, Theresa struggled with a decision on what to do for many weeks. She knew that to bring her mother into her home would create more conflict in her already tenuous marriage and drive her over the edge. After much angst, Theresa decided to put her mother in a nursing home. Six months later she was dead and Theresa was unable to forgive herself for her decision. She dreaded the nights, fearing her mother would be there in her dreams as she had been in life - angry and shaming. While she knew she had made the right decision considering her life circumstances, Theresa was unable to quiet down the blaming daytime thoughts that she was responsible for her mother's death. "If I had let her come live with me, she'd still be alive," she'd tell me. The self-critical, blaming voice that Theresa had internalized early in childhood left her feeling that she would be burdened with this guilt for the rest of her life.

Theresa's haven was the ocean. Whenever she was worn down by the tasks of raising five children, depressed by the lack of closeness with her husband or worried about money, she would go to the ocean. Walking the beach would help her to have the courage and stamina to re-enter her life with a sense of renewal. She would even go on rainy days and sit in her car with the window open listening to the comforting sound of the pounding surf. When Theresa began to talk with me about her heavy burden of guilt, I asked her if she had been spending time in her healing place, at the ocean. She looked surprised and said she hadn't been there in quite some time. She had "forgotten" about her friend the ocean. I wondered aloud if she were punishing herself some more by not doing what she knew would help her to heal. Encouraging Theresa to return to her sanctuary during this difficult time, I talked with her about the ocean as a powerful archetypal image of Mother. "The Divine Mother," I told Theresa, "looks on us with compassion and forgives us our human limitations. You need to open yourself to taking in this forgiveness and feeling it inside of you." I suggested to Theresa that she use the mantra or prayer "Please Forgive Me" and repeat it to herself while at the water's edge.

Initially when Theresa returned to the ocean, the pounding of the waves seemed angry, as if they were bearers of her mother's message. But over time, as her projective process quieted down, the sound of the waves softened until one day an image from childhood came spontaneously into her mind. There she was, a young girl, maybe four- or five-years-old in a pool, her mother holding her tenderly. Theresa began to cry quietly. She had forgotten this more loving side of her mother. After the emergence of this memory, she began to feel a sense of forgiveness inside herself. She continued her sojourns to the ocean, and over time, the feeling grew stronger. As Theresa was able to come to herself with a sense of compassion and loving kindness, she also gradually developed feelings of compassion for her mother and her own human limitations.

The most important aspect of the preparation phase of self-forgiveness is to create an attitude of openness, an inner receptivity into which forgiveness can enter. That is why we recommend, as Theresa did, spending a lot of time returning again and again to your forgiveness place in nature. Nature helps to create that receptivity by her welcoming invitation, by her nonjudgmental presence and by offering herself as sanctuary. Prayer, simple prayer, will also help to prepare a receptive space into which forgiveness can enter.

Different people pray in different ways. By tradition we may think of prayer as the instructive prayers that we learned as children in church or temple. For some people the structure of this kind of prayer is necessary and helpful. But when we talk about using prayer in self-forgiveness work we generally talk about private prayer, simple, direct prayer that comes from the soul. It does not matter to whom we pray, God, a Higher Power, or the Universal Consciousness.

It only matters that we pray, simply and directly. Joan Borysenko tells us that:

> Pain yearns for comfort . . . When we are absolutely miserable, prayer is no longer a dry, rote repetition. It becomes a living and vibrant cry for help. It becomes authentic. In pain we . . . reach a new state of intimacy that comes from talking to God in our own way, saying what's in our heart.[25]

When we do this work with people, we give them several index cards with simple words or prayers written on them:

FORGIVENESS

PLEASE FORGIVE ME

HELP ME TO FORGIVE MYSELF

I FORGIVE ME

We encourage them to spend some time each day, in their nature place if possible, with the word or prayer that they intuitively connect with, saying the prayer several times, focusing on their breathing, repeating the prayer . . . and after a series of these, allowing whatever thoughts, feelings or images may come into the mind. Sometimes it may feel as if nothing is happening, but if you continue with the daily prayer time, eventually a place of receptivity to forgiveness will begin to open. From our prayers we will gain courage. But we also will experience times of great darkness, when we feel we do not have any strength or courage, only a deep yearning to be forgiven. At these times, more than others, we need to be prayerful. Prayerfulness, as Larry Dossey describes it, is different than prayer. It is an active acceptance, a willingness to be present to the mystery of things, to tolerate the unknown and honor the rightness of whatever happens.[26] For some of us, the kind of personal prayer and this prayerful attitude does not happen easily in a church. Church is usually associated with specific prayers, liturgy and ritual, not personal dialogue with God. This personal dialogue, we have found, is often more possible in the church that God built - nature. Time spent in nature can be a sanctuary experience that creates an opening to the divine, within and without. We are able to be less guarded, less self-conscious in nature. We can become more Self-conscious, more connected to our deeper Self.

❦

After awareness and preparation, the next phase of self-forgiveness is emergence. This is what happened to Theresa when the image from childhood came back to her. Feelings of self-forgiveness began to emerge. Just as so many of us begin to come to life again when the light of spring breaks through the darkness of winter, as self-forgiveness happens, we begin to emerge from the darkness of guilt. The "dark night of the soul" has ended and we begin to move on in our lives. We have found that the conscious use of imagery is the most potent way of facilitating the emergence of self-forgiveness. Because images bypass our tendency to intellectualize, they are able to connect us directly with the deeper parts of Self and touch our hearts and souls in a more powerful way than words. Through a process of meditation and visualization we can connect with an image of compassion and forgiveness that has personal meaning for us. For some people, images arise spontaneously during meditation. For others, a specific image may be chosen beforehand to use. Many people find very traditional religious or spiritual images, such as Jesus or Buddha or Mary most helpful. Others may use a particular power animal, the Tree of Life or an image of the Universal Heart. Some use the image of a person in their life who has been a source of compassion and forgiveness, perhaps a parent or grandparent, relative, friend, teacher or mentor. Still others, who have never experienced forgiveness from anyone in their lives, draw upon some personal representation of an archetypal image. Whatever the image, it must embody the qualities of compassion and forgiveness.

##  Bill

Ralph, a serious and complex man in his mid-thirties, was abandoned by his father when he was four and left in the hands of his psychotic mother. They lived on welfare until he was an adult. I remember one session with Ralph, an early winter evening, when the radiator in my office was hissing and sputtering with the sound of heat rising in the ancient pipes. I apologized for the intrusive noise. Ralph smiled, remembering the long, cold winter nights of his childhood. "It's a sweet sound to me," he said. Frequent evictions, inadequate food, the unpredictable tornadoes of rage and paranoid ramblings of his mother and the physical abuse of older siblings left Ralph struggling to maintain his sanity.

When he was 12, Ralph had physically abused his nine-year-old sister. While he had asked for forgiveness in adulthood and she had forgiven him, Ralph was unable to stop his own constant self-recriminations. His heart was heavy with the burden of his guilt. During one session in which his guilt was unusually strong, I had Ralph close his eyes and, after some relaxation breathing, allow an image of compassion and forgiveness to come into his mind's eye. I told him to trust whatever image came from his Higher Self. Ralph immediately saw himself sitting at the feet of Hans Christian Anderson. He felt a warmth, understanding, and compassion emanating from him, and, while no words were exchanged, he took those feelings inside himself.

After the imagery, Ralph shared with me that, as a child, Anderson's stories had provided him with a source of fatherly guidance and kindness. For him, Hans Christian Anderson was a benevolent, reliable, gently source of male wisdom and compassion. With all of the malevolent people in his childhood, he was in desperate need of this. It made sense that, now, when he needed to forgive himself, this early image would return as the archetypal Wise Old Man. With encouragement from me, Ralph continued to use the image of himself at the feet of Hans Christian Anderson, taking in the feelings of compassion and forgiveness. Over time, he was able to release some of his old guilt.

***

Using the breath is a simple way to begin a meditation to find an image of compassion and forgiveness. By following the breath, letting thoughts and other distractions come and go, and bringing our attention back to the breath, we can connect more easily with our inner experience. Try this:

> Bring your attention to your breathing. Be aware of your breath as you breathe in through your nose, then as you breathe out.

If thoughts come into your mind, or you notice sounds from the outside, just notice them and bring your attention back to your breath. After a few moments of following your breath, go into your imagination and allow an image to emerge that represents deep compassion and forgiveness. Trust what emerges, whether it is the image of a person, an animal, an image from nature. Your psyche knows what you need to heal. If you have chosen a specific image that you want to work with, allow that image to come into your mind. Imagine your personal image of forgiveness in detail. As you breathe in, think of yourself as drawing into you the compassion that is embodied in this symbol. As you breathe out, imagine yourself letting go the guilt and fear. Breathe in compassion and forgiveness; breathe out guilt and fear. Say a simple prayer if you like, Please forgive me; Help me to forgive myself. Breathe in compassion and forgiveness; breathe out guilt and fear.

Once we have an image of a forgiving presence, our task is to go to our sanctuary, our sacred place in nature, close our eyes and visualize the image. And then let the deeper Self do the rest, trusting whatever happens with the image. This is the hardest thing for us, to trust that some other part of us intrinsically knows how to heal us, to let go of our conscious controls and permit the deep Self to do its work. After the preparation work that we have done, the use of imagery and visualization will help to create an opening into which forgiveness will enter. In its own time.

## Jeanne

I have done lots of self-forgiveness work over the years. Usually it is not planned. Something in my life triggers old feelings of guilt or regret and there I am, back in the process, needing to forgive myself again. Each time, I am able to forgive myself more deeply. This story of forgiveness happened several years ago when Bill and I had gone to the country for a weekend. I did not expect to be doing this kind of psychological and spiritual work - we had gone there to get away from work! But, as we have said, forgiveness has its own timetable. We can't predict when we need to enter into the process, we can only try to remain open and be prepared. Had I closed myself down to this time, I would have missed one of the most profound healing experiences in my life. I have returned to my journal entries of those few days to try and capture the immediacy and depth of the experience.

*The Mother cries rivers of tears for the pain of all her children.* These words echo through my mind as I think back on those few days:

I am sitting on a rock in the middle of an open field. For days I have felt a pain in my heart. Now the pain overwhelms me and I am crying. Crying for the pain I have brought into this world, especially to my children. Dear Mother, how can I ever be forgiven for such great pain. I am crying so hard that my heart will break. I do not feel you near me, Mother, though I know you are all around me. It is dark. The night wind is cool, caressing me, wrapping 'round my shoulders. I know you are here, yet I can barely feel you. My tears are endless. They grip my chest. I am sure they will never stop. And my heart shall break for all the pain it carries. The night is overcast. A gentle rain begins to fall. I sit in the dark on this rock in the open field. I am sure my Mother and all the angels are crying with me. The rain is a comfort to me. Through my tears, I talk to my children. *I love you so very much, I cannot bear that I have caused you pain. That my choices to end my marriage and break up our family have meant that you have had to see and hear things you should not. That you've experienced feelings beyond your capacity to understand, and that you've had to grow up too soon.* So much darkness all around me, the rain falling gently, my tears, endless, my heart breaking from the pain. And then the sky begins to clear. Powerful feelings and seemingly disconnected thoughts rush into me. I remember talks I have had

135

with others about self-forgiveness. I don't feel deserving of forgiveness right now. I don't feel worthy. But we don't need to be deserving or worthy, I tell myself as I've told others, not believing my own words. We are just forgiven. The sky above me is now a mass of stars, so beautiful it takes my breath away. Just forgiven . . . I want to feel this, but my heart cannot believe it is possible. I want to make amends. Can I ever make amends? Can I ever give back to my children parts of childhood that have been taken away? I think not. The pain I have caused is carried in the hearts of my little ones and will always be a part of them. I wonder if there are some wounds we can never make direct amends for and, yet, the desire to do so is very strong. The small self, the self that is out in the world, needs to make amends. The other, The Higher Self or the Soul, just forgives. The Soul is beyond the small self and does not need amends. Both are true, I think to myself. The need to make amends and the need to be "just forgiven." Perhaps we make amends indirectly sometimes, not to the ones we've hurt but through others. Perhaps through my work, I make amends, by helping another mother to be with her own children in a different way, or by mothering a child other than my own. It's like gratitude, I think. Sometimes we can't repay directly a kindness that has been shown us but we can show our gratitude by passing that kindness along to another. Maybe making amends works in a similar way and this is as important as opening myself fully to "just forgiveness." Finally, with these thought, my tears subside.

For days I am disconnected from "normal" life. I am in another state of consciousness, a chrysalis, focused fully on this inner task of self-forgiveness. I am grateful that we are in the country, that I do not have to contend with the mundane things of life and can give myself over fully to this internal process. For days, I am having thoughts and images about forgiveness and "Mother." I am not sure what they're about. Images fill me of my own mother holding me in my pain, offering me comfort and consolation; images of me lying in a river, the waters of forgiveness washing over me. More thoughts pour in. They are not fully clear but I know they are connected in some way to this whole process. In my meditation, I see that Mother Earth is forgiving. We cut down the trees and pollute the waters, and in doing so we wound her. But if we recognize our wounding and stop, she begins to heal and in the healing she forgives us. The trees grow once again; the waters run clear after a time. Something is connected here for me. Something about Mother, about nature as Mother, about the forgiving nature of Mother.

Somehow, if nature can forgive us through her healing, then through my own healing I must be forgivable. I feel the truth of this.

❧

I am playing in the stream, climbing on the rocks, sliding down mossy inclines. I am drawn after a while to a spot that is different from the rest, like a grotto in the midst of the stream. Although I have not been consciously looking, this is the place, I know intuitively, that I have been looking for. I kneel down in the water among the rocks and let the water wash over me. I am sobbing and asking for forgiveness. Mother, please forgive me. Forgive me for my betrayals of my children. I feel a peacefulness, even as I cry, that I have not felt in a long time. This is the place I need to be. For a long time, I kneel in the stream, the waters of forgiveness washing over me. The voice of the stream comforts me.

*The Mother cries rivers of tears for the pain of all her children,* she says. I know her tears are for my pain and for my children's pain. Forgive me, Mother, I say to her, for my betrayals of my children.

❧

I sit in meditation now alongside the stream, surrounded by forest, a beam of sunlight washing over me, the voice of the river's comforting words washing through me. *The Mother cries rivers of tears for the pain of all her children. I am in the Mother's womb; her waters wash over me with forgiveness. In this woods near the river, in this crevice of the stony mountain, I am in the womb of my Mother. And I know that I am forgiven.*

※※※※※

While I was in this forgiveness process, I did not think about why it was happening in this way. I just knew that I needed to surrender to what began while I sat in the field on the rock in the dark. All of the preparation I had done over time had created an opening for this work to happen at this time, for whatever reason. In self-forgiveness work, it is essential to be openly receptive to the inexplicable and surrender to the mystery. Yet, by nature, I want to know the meaning of things. That part of me won't let the experience just be. So I muse about it. Why had it happened at this time in this way? Certainly my deeper Self knew I was ready and took advantage of this prolonged time in nature to move me into this process. I felt the presence of nature so powerfully and in a definitely feminine way. She was present to me each step along the way. My wounding was as a mother. Did I need to feel the presence and forgiveness of a Mother greater than I? Did nature connect me to the Great Mother, the "divine feminine" that resides both outside and inside of me? Certainly my image of God had been predominantly that of the male, punitive and condemning God that I had learned about through Church and family. But that was not the God-presence I felt. Perhaps nature connected me to a compassionate, forgiving Divine Mother, awakened the archetypal Great Mother, long dormant in the consciousness of my deeper Self. And through this image and the experience of her presence, I was forgiven. I speculate, attempt to explain the inexplicable mystery of forgiveness.

Each of us needs to trust our own process as we first open ourselves to self-forgiveness. Forgiveness will occur for each of us in different ways, at different times, in different nature settings. As feelings of self-forgiveness emerge over time, we enter the fourth stage of this process, deepening. The deepening of our feelings of self-forgiveness is ongoing and occurs as we return to this work intermittently through our lives. As the feelings deepen, our burden of guilt will continue to be lifted.

# Gardens

In 1976, Marilyn Barrett, a psychotherapist and photographer, was diagnosed with multiple sclerosis. Deciding that if she was going to die, the thing she most wanted to do was to create a garden, Marilyn quit her job, moved near the ocean and started gardening. "As my garden grew up around me," she explains in her book, *Creating Eden, the garden as a healing space*, "I began to change." After a year of gardening, her symptoms began to disappear. Doctors said that her original diagnosis must have been wrong. Who knows? In the realm of physical, psychological and spiritual healing, it is important to have a healthy respect for the mysterious. As she worked her garden, a number of profound physical and psychological changes occurred, including the lifting of her depression.

"As my garden began to take tentative shape," Marilyn writes, "my psyche, too, began to form an image of where I was in my life."[27]

We could say that her deeper Self "knew" how Marilyn needed to heal herself or that perhaps she was "remembering" a knowledge that is part of our collective unconscious. Or some other explanation. What is clear from her story and from others' stories is the powerful healing potential of gardens and the process of gardening. While many people seem to know this intuitively and are drawn to their gardens in times of emotional or physical depletion, to make this knowledge conscious can increase the efficacy of the garden as a healing place.

Nature has always played a part in physical and emotional healing. Most of our modern medicines have their origins in some plant, root, herb or other

substance from the natural world. In Victorian times, "hysterical" women were often sent to the country for a "cure." During the terrible tuberculosis outbreak in the early part of this century, patients from the cities, including Jeanne's maternal grandmother, were often sent to a sanatorium in the country to be in the clean, fresh air. And when hospitals were first instituted, medicinal and healing gardens were an essential element. In Padua, Italy for example, since the sixteenth century, the hospital there has been celebrated for its garden. In the United States, the oldest medicinal garden, dating from 1879, is located at Friends Hospital in Philadelphia. A greenhouse on the grounds of this psychiatric facility was utilized specifically for horticultural therapy with patients. The hospital also had a unique policy of providing care for nonpaying patients in exchange for work done on the hospital gardens. Old records show that doctors reported that those patients who performed this gardening work recovered more quickly. The hospital continues to include horticultural therapy as an integral part of the treatment regimen for about one third of its patients.

Recently Topler Delany, a landscape architect, has become a leader in reviving the "lost tradition" of healing gardens.[28] In the late 1980s, Topler learned that she had breast cancer. Wandering the halls and waiting rooms of a San Francisco hospital, she was unable to find a quiet place where she could absorb this devastating news. That experience provided her life with a new direction. Since then she has been designing medicinal gardens where patients can go for quiet contemplation, sanctuary and emotional renewal. One of her projects is the Marin Healing Garden at Marin Hospital in California. Patients awaiting or receiving chemotherapy and radiation treatments can look out over an atrium of brilliant flowers against a backdrop of natural stone and redwood walls. The garden is filled with medicinal plants chosen specifically because they are sources of drugs for chemotherapy. Patients are given cards that explain the healing folklore of these plants as well as the scientific basis for their role in fighting cancer. The garden contains herbs, such as St. John's Wort, passionflower, feverfew, horsetail and coneflower, that are useful in dealing with other physical and emotional effects of cancer.

And so, while the tradition of gardens as healing places is a long one, our present consciousness of their potential to aid in the process of physical, emotional and spiritual healing is lagging. Perhaps by sharing some of our patients' stories, we can shed further light on the emotional and spiritual aspects of this process.

 Jeanne

Gardening, quite naturally, has long been used as a metaphor for psychological and spiritual growth. As a therapist, its use is quite perfect and ordinary at the same time, and so well-suited to certain people in particular. As I became more conscious of the healing power of gardens, I began listening for stories my patients would tell about their gardens. Quite often someone would talk about working in their garden or caring for their yard and I would be struck by their enthusiasm and love for these tasks. Cleaning up the yard, preparing flower beds while observing the emergence of last year's bulbs, planting new seeds or seedlings was not work for these people. It was a labor of love, a time for quiet reflection and focused attention. I began to use the garden as a metaphor for our therapeutic work more often. I would suggest starting a garden or going into an already existing garden with a consciousness of how the garden and the tasks of gardening reflect the inner work that we do. I sometimes think of myself as a gardener of the psyche. I teach my patients the skills necessary for tending their own inner garden: how to first clear the ground of weeds and debris; how to till the soil, water and nourish it; how to add compost and turn it over and over until it is rich and brown and ready for seeds. Then we plant seeds together. We try to find the ones most suited to their particular soil. Some seeds take easily; others wither and die or do not take at all. The seeds that do take root, sprout, grow and blossom are the ones that are just right for this particular garden.

So many of us have had our inner gardens planted for us. Well-intentioned parents, teachers and other important adults are really the first caretakers of our intrapsychic gardens. But when they are emotionally needy, psychologically underdeveloped or spiritually undernourished, the seeds they plant so often have more to do with their own needs than ours. My soil (soul) may be best suited to a garden of blazing wildflowers, but if my parents are insistent on cultivating rigid rows of evenly placed, greenhouse-raised seedlings, I'm in trouble. This kind of a garden is totally unsuited to who I am and I will not thrive in these conditions. Not having the modeling I need to know how to tend a wildflower garden, I may spend many of my adult years feeling like a misfit without a place in this world, a wild daisy among rows of staid marigolds.

---

Separated after nine years of marriage, Joyce spends weekends working in her yard. Her ex-husband, Troy, had pulled trees and bushes from the woods behind their house and planted them in small, scattered islands in their front yard. He gave no thought to their placement. "Will this grow well here? Will it get enough sunlight? Will it enhance the beauty of our home?" These questions never occurred to him. Many of the trees, ripped as they were from their proper home, died over time. Troy also dug a pond in the backyard and put fish in it. The fish, too, died and Joyce was left with an acrid-smelling hole in the ground. None of this work was thought through. No planning or attention was given to what might work best in their soil. Now, with the divorce final and Joyce caring for the house alone, she is digging up, raking, removing rocks and transplanting. She is frustrated by the disarray that has been left to her and resentful about the amount of work she has to do to repair the damage done by Troy.

"It takes me a whole day to do one small flower bed. I'm exhausted when I finish. But then I just stand there looking at it, thinking how pretty it looks. My neighbors probably think I'm crazy, staring at this one little flower bed, but I feel so good!"

Joyce has worked hard. In the eighteen months since she separated from Troy, she has grown from a whining, victimized girl to a self-confident woman. She used to walk with her shoulders slumped inwards, as if to offer some protection to her heart. She is now in touch with her vulnerability and willing to again risk her heart in love. She has blossomed and blossomed again during our work together. But, as happens with all of us at certain times, Joyce is frustrated that her life is not yet where she wants it to be. After exploring these feelings, I tell her that her work in the yard is a metaphor for the inner work she is doing. In her yard, she is bringing order to the chaos left by Troy. As he did with the trees and pond, Troy never thought about the impact upon Joyce of anything he did. Now she has to clear away the psychic debris and damage of years of emotional abuse and neglect. As she does this clearing out, preparation for a new self and a more fulfilling life is happening all the time. But the work is long and arduous, just like her work outside. It takes a whole day to pull up some bushes, remove rocks, rake the ground and plant some flowers in a small area. It has taken almost two years from the time of her separation for Joyce to get to an emotional place where she finally feels like a good person, deserving of recognition in her work, and worthy of a loving, thoughtful partner in her life. But just as gardens need ongoing care and attention with each season, we must do the same for the continuing growth of our own inner garden, the psyche.

As Joyce works in her yard and watches her flower beds take shape, she becomes more aware of process, that neither flowers nor people blossom overnight. Over time, she relaxes into the process and is more patient and gentle with herself. She learns that there are times of difficult, concentrated labor and periods of just waiting. She begins to notice the seasons, too. New seeds are planted and emerge as young seedlings in the spring. In summer, the seedlings need tending, nourishing and support to grow into healthy plants. In fall, we harvest the fruits of our hard work. In winter, when the land lies fallow and nothing at all seems to be happening, much preparation is going on beneath the earth.

We, too, have our psychological seasons, though they need not correspond to the seasons in nature. It's important to trust our own timing. Even in the natural world, seasons vary. Witness the miracle of the Christmas cactus. Each Christmastime, when much of the rest of the plant world is in the dormancy of winter, it appears resplendent in the glory of its spring. Each plant, each creature has its own time, its own season. So, too, with each of us. In our inner spring, seeds of a new self are planted. After a period of gestation, the seeds begin to emerge in the form of new behaviors, deepened compassion for self and others, less "black and white" thinking and a greater tolerance for the "gray," or some other new ways of being in the world. These young "self-seedlings" then need to be fed, nourished and supported in order to keep growing into stronger, synthesized parts of Self. During this summer season, other parts of self may need to be weeded out, or we may periodically need transplanting in our work or relationships. Sometime later, we reap the autumn harvest of our hard inner work in the shape of a more fully formed, more "real" Self. And then, just as in our garden, we begin again the preparation for the seeds to be sown next spring. Time and more time passes and on the surface nothing seems to be happening. This is our inner winter. We have done all this work, some change has occurred, but now we are stagnating; nothing seems to be happening. While on the surface this is what we feel, inside much preparation is taking place. Thoughts, feelings, experiences and insights that have been turned over again and again act as the mulch for our inner soil, preparing our psyche for future seeds that will be planted.

Terri, a woman in her fifties, is not a gardener herself but the memory of her mother and her garden was a powerful catalyst for Terri's psychological growth. Recently she was talking about how difficult it is for her to take time for herself. She always puts her husband's and children's needs before her own, like her own mother did. To do otherwise feels selfish to Terri.

"My mother was such a great mom," Terri says wistfully. "She never took any time for herself. With four kids and my father to take care of, she was always busy. I guess that when she took her bath at night, she was trying to get some alone time, as I think about it now. But I would often walk in on her, plop myself down on the floor and talk with her. We had such great talks then. It was a special time in our relationship."

Terri was tearful as she remembered these important moments with her mother. "I wonder now if she resented my intruding into her time. It would be so much easier for me to take time for myself if I knew that my mother had taken time for herself." While her mother was a powerful model of caretaking, Terri lacked any kind of strong modeling of how to nurture her own need for Self time. Then, amidst her tears, a memory floated into Terri's mind of her mother in her garden. She recalled how much she loved spending time in her garden and how she always did it alone.

"She never asked us for help. In fact, as I'm thinking about it now, she didn't want our help." As Terri recalled, her mother was never tired or irritable when she came in from the garden and never complained about all that hard work. "In fact," Terri said, "she was just the opposite - peaceful, relaxed and more energetic. She was usually smiling when she came from gardening. I never could understand it. I would hate all that work, but she loved it. She loved all the seasons, too, as long as she could be outside doing something, anything, in her garden."

For Terri's mother, her garden was a place of sanctuary, a refuge from her endless caretaking tasks. It was not work for her in the sense of drudgery, but a time to nourish her deeper Self. Working in the soil and tending her flowers and vegetables was a kind of emotional fertilizer. That is why she was so cheerful and energetic afterwards. Remembering the image of her mother in her garden provided Terri with the model she needed for taking Self time without feeling guilty.

Sarah also has a garden. Hers is a garden of wildflowers, roses, annuals and perennials that she has been cultivating over the last ten years. She never gave much thought to what this garden might have meant in terms of her own growth process, except to know that she loves working in it. She loves feeling her hands in the soil, trimming, transplanting and sitting peacefully among her flowers surveying the beauty that her hard work has wrought.

Sarah began to tell me about her garden during the time when we were doing some self-forgiveness work together. She had had an abortion years earlier and suffered tremendous guilt and anguish. At the time of the abortion, Sarah felt strongly that she was not emotionally equipped to raise any more children than the three she already had. The abortion was a matter of survival. As with many women who have had abortions, she knew that she had made the right life decision for what was happening at the time. But, as time went on and her complexity of thinking and feeling developed, Sarah felt that, with the abortion, she had wrongly ended the life of a little soul. Her guilt was overwhelming. As her garden was a place of real peace for her, I encouraged Sarah to go into it more consciously, to spend time there as she worked to forgive herself. One day she told me that she realized that she had begun to plant her garden just after having the abortion. Perhaps, she mused, the garden was a way to bring something to life in amends for the life she felt she had taken. We were both struck by the symbolic nature of this act and by the awesome power of the unconscious to urge us toward healing. However, the healing power of Sarah's garden increased dramatically with her deepened awareness of the garden as her sanctuary and place of healing.

As she worked through her feelings of sadness, self-anger and guilt about the abortion, Sarah would spend hours of solitary time in her garden gently tending and nourishing, not only her flowers, but her wounded self. As time passed, she was more able to forgive herself and felt a deep sense of compassion for herself at an earlier time in her life.

In her garden healing place, Sarah would move deep into the rich earth of her psyche, tending, tilling, fertilizing as her hands worked the moist soil around her flowers. Toward the end of our work together, that last summer, Sarah would bring me frequent updates on her garden. Fully conscious now of its healing power, she would spend long hours in it when she needed nurturing and healing in other aspects of her life also. Over time, her garden evolved in fascinating ways. One day, just before our last session together, Sarah sat in her garden and wrote about each variety of flower and how it came to represent an important person in her life:

I have been in my garden for hours today and have lost all concept of space and time. My uncle died a few months ago. His gift to me was his appreciation of nature: the smells, the sounds, the colors and textures of things. We would spend time outside just sitting and listening. Today seemed a good day to visit him in my garden . . . and listen. In that quiet time within my own mind, while weeding barefoot in the soil, I was introduced to so much understanding of my own life. I connected to the people in my life through my garden.

Jessie, my daughter, is the beautiful rose. She stands tall and beautiful yet very much unapproachable to me. Roses are a major part of my garden, as she has been a major part of my life . . . a mixture of beauty and pain. Dew drops on the petals are my tears, for if I pruned them or cut them to bring inside, I would always feel the thorns. Maybe they are best left to grow in their own way. For a second I become the rose, knowing the feeling of wanting to live my own life.

There, in the exact middle of the garden, is an evergreen. It is a thorny bush. It's my dad, with his omnipresence, somehow always threatening me with his power, shading the violets from the sunlight. Once a year, I clip that evergreen and for the rest of the growing season the sharp thorns find their way into my feet. I gave him power over my thoughts; he only meant to protect me. Maybe he wanted me to grow to be a thorny bush like him. Today, I forgive him.

The daylilies grow like weeds, deep rooted and towering over all. That's Aunt Dot, the family matriarch, regal and needing to look down on all those around her. Her roots reach out, trying to intertwine with the adjoining flowers. It seems similar to the way I try to keep my family so close to me, while in my heart, I know they need to grow from their own roots. Her pride is so evident as she makes us aware that she is always right. I try to dig these roots out and lessen their presence but they keep growing back. Is it my own pride I see here? It is a lesson in humility I need for myself. I fight her pride each time she visits, as my own pride seems as strong. Today, I will accept her for who she is.

Polka dot plants . . . little pink polka dots on green leaves. They are Aunt Lil. Cheerful, colorful little branches sway in the breeze; little dancers that bring a smile to my face, as she does. She always helps me to see the better side of things. There will always be pain in life and there will always be joy. Accept one and enjoy the other. Separate the feelings. If you name it pain you will cry, but if you call it joy it can be uplifting. Today I call it joy.

In each section of may garden, there is a Dusty Miller plant. That is Jeanne, my therapist. My eye is drawn to the silver plant. It has no flowers but its beauty and uniqueness is what I seek in my own life. It represents strength and understanding, always reflecting the sun's light; always inviting me into its stability. It is centered among other flowers in the area, as she helps me to center myself. It is not adorned; it is self-confident as I wish to be. Yet, without it there, the other flowers would not be as beautiful. The silver tone brings out the beauty of the other flowers that would not have been noticed without her presence. Her presence in my life made me see the beauty in myself, something I failed to find on my own. Silver, the color of a mirror. She holds the mirror up for me to see my own reflection and it comes with the invitation to step inside, to find the dimensions of me. It has been a rewarding journey.

Ah, the marigolds: Maggie, my truest friend, ever-blooming as our friendship has been, as fragrant as her personality. Short ones and tall ones signifying our friendship's up and downs. We have seen each other through love and anger, good times and bad times. Shared our thoughts and dreams, as many as there are tiny petals on each bloom. Makes me appreciate a good friendship. You always seemed so much better at everything than I was. You would never take responsibility for my feelings of being so jealous of your beauty and wisdom. I let my jealousy get in the way of our closeness sometimes. I see that in the face of the marigold now. I smile back at you, sitting here in the dirt. We are both human, neither of us infallible. You treated me as an equal, yet in my own mind I put you on a pedestal that I thought I could never reach. I regret that. I sit here looking at you, eye-to-eye, putting jealously aside and feeling my own worth as a woman who has the gift of a true friend. Our friendship will grow even closer through the coming years because I have learned to grow.

The coleus, shades of red and orange, bright yet shaded with hues of brown and umber, strong yet not without its hidden sensitivity. That's you, Dave, my husband, my lover, my friend. Each petal spotted with the flare of you. Your background color so consistent with your loyalty. Your velvet touch when I need consoling. Large leaves so much like your broad shoulders I need to lean on. You have taught me to find my independence. You gave me trust and sent me on to explore life by encouraging me to go back to school. You loved me enough to have your children. Our children. You accepted and loved me even through my worst behavior. You told me I was beautiful when I felt my ugliest. And in your eyes I saw the princess of the castle. I tried to help you see the prince when you looked back. You taught me to find my own happiness, and enjoyed when I found things that appealed to me. You have an unconditional love that expects nothing from me in return. I wish to achieve that total acceptance you have of all things. The coleus, melding into the background colors of my garden, and so enmeshed in my life. The coleus, not so noticeable, maybe taken for granted, maybe needing more than a glance from me once in a while. The rose took so much of my time. I failed to see that you, too, needed nourishment. You have such patience. I'll make time now to give you the gifts you generously gave me.

The sun is setting. I have been in this garden for hours. My mother . . . where is my mother? I sit here on the warm soil and quietly listen. "I am the Earth you sit on; you are the garden. I have been here always to comfort you, to nourish you, to help you see you are the roses, the thorny bushes, marigolds, dusty miller, lilies and even the weeds. In each you've found what you needed to grow. You found your strengths and your weaknesses here. The weeds may be deep rooted as your faults are, but learn from them; pick them and lay them on my earth. Know them. They are great fertilizer. Knowing you faults and accepting them can only enhance the beauty of each flower that grows within you."

For each of these women, the garden meant something very different, something that fit their own individual journeys perfectly. Each found some measure of healing and some degree of growth through the experience of their gardens or, as in Terri's case, through the memory of her mother in her garden. For each, bringing consciousness to the task, to the memory, to the place itself, increased its efficacy as a facilitator of healing.

For so many of us, time spent in the garden is unconscious. We know that to be there with our hands in the dirt, tending plants, turning the soil, our bodies in the warmth of the sun or the cool of the shade, is beneficial but we are unable to articulate why. In some cultures, when a child is born a tree is planted. As the child grows into an adult she regularly visits the tree, tending it. The tree and the child have a relationship. A conscious connection with the natural world begins early and is fostered throughout her lifetime. The tree and the adult grow old together.

In our culture, we are increasingly alienated from nature and so our healing in the garden and our relationship with the plants and trees happens "accidentally" through the subconscious urging of the Higher Self. If we can begin to enter our gardens with a new consciousness, then the potential for healing increases significantly. We and the garden – and subsequently the Earth – benefit from bringing an added dimension to our gardening tasks. Whether we begin to bring a more mindful attention to our gardening, or view our garden work as a mutual healing relationship – "I sustain the garden, the garden sustains me" – whether our garden is a potted plant on a window sill or an acre of flowers and vegetables, the essential ingredient, in addition to water and sunlight, is our conscious intent.

# PATH

## 🌸 Bill

We all look for models, mentors and teachers on our spiritual journey. At this time in my own journey, I look back into history for people I consider "nature mystics." By this I mean those whose spiritual journey has included significant periods of solitary time in nature that has allowed them direct experience of God, the Absolute, or the One. I first think of the great spiritual teachers Jesus, Buddha and Lao-tzu. Then, St. Francis, Hildegaard von Bingen and Meister Eckhart. Next I think of Kahlil Gibran, Thoreau Emerson and Muir. These nature mystics from various times and traditions have all incorporated their experiences of nature in their efforts to teach us. I aspire to be like them, to walk a similar path.

Historically, each of the great religious traditions has its mystical aspect that points to nature as a way of knowing God. In Hinduism, there is a reverence for all other forms of life because of the belief that the Supreme Being was incarnated in the form of various species and that, in the cycle of birth and rebirth a person may come back as an animal, bird or some other creature. The early Buddhist communities lived with great respect and gratitude "comfortably in nature." In the Sutta-Nipata, one of the earliest Buddhist texts, the Buddha says, "Know ye the grasses and the trees . . . then know ye the worms, and the moths, and the different sorts of ant . . ."[29]

In the Sephardic tradition, some of the great sages were also nature poets. They saw "nature as beautiful and worthy in and of itself – and also as a path toward the most beautiful and worthy of all, God."

## God Everywhere

Wherever I turn my eyes, around on Earth
or to the heavens
I see You in the field of stars
I see You in the yield of the land
in every breath and sound, a blade of grass,
a simple flower, an echo of Your holy Name

(Abraham Ibu Ezra)[30]

The Kabbalists also viewed the contemplation of nature as a "path toward the love and contemplation of God." One Jewish mystical tradition included daily outdoor meditation and the mystics of Safed developed a Seder to

celebrate the presence of God in nature. Baal Shem Tov, the founder of Hasidim, said that "a man should consider himself as a worm, and all other small animals as his companions in the world, for all of them are created."[30]

At this time in my life, nature is my primary spiritual path. Each morning I wake up early and walk a short distance into the woods to a grove of fir trees. Interestingly, I have to walk behind a Christian church to get to my sanctuary. It is only now, as I reflect on this, that I am consciously aware of the symbolism of that. I was raised a Christian, but now I am outside of that traditional spiritual path. In the woods I sit under a huge evergreen and do my meditation before entering the world of work. I feel so blessed to have this grove of trees available to me every day. So much of daily life is lived in exile from nature. We live in cities of concrete and asphalt, in suburban homes of sheetrock and manicured lawns, in rooms with TV and computer screens. We work in boxes called offices breathing recirculated, toxic air often without even a window to give visual access to the natural world. This exile is so insidious we don't even realize it's happening. It feels normal. This past winter we had a number of snow storms that forced businesses and schools to close. People had free time to go outside and romp in the magical play land that nature had created. I was astounded and saddened at how few people were outside walking, throwing snowballs or making angels in the snow. Where was everyone? Inside watching videos and playing computer games? This wonderful opportunity to be outside and play and connect with nature was passed up by so many. Our alienation from nature, from the outside world, seems to be increasing. I remember as a child that when it snowed lots of people were outside. This alienation from the natural world is contributing powerfully to our alienation from our deep Self and from God. By beginning my day in the woods, I am returning to and remembering my origin as a creature of nature, one of God's creations. It seems to me that a central aspect of the journey of the nature mystic is a returning home, a remembering our ancient connection to creation, a connection that has been severed.

In response to this urge to be in nature as my spiritual path, this last year I have arranged my schedule so that one long morning each week I take a walk in a local wildlife refuge. On different days I think of the time as a Sabbat in the Jewish sense, or a service in the Christian tradition, or a morning of mindfulness in the Buddhist way. I bring with me a knapsack filled with a towel to put on the ground for meditation, a thermos of herbal tea, a piece of fruit, a small loaf of wheat bread and my writing pad. I enter the sacred space and say a prayer of gratitude for the time and place away from the madness of contemporary life. Then I begin to walk, responding to the needs of my deeper Self, the beckoning of the spirit and other creatures. Some mornings are filled with a number of meditations. Other times a lot of spontaneous chanting or songs emerge. Sometimes much sensual contact with the trees, flowers or grasses occurs. Sometimes I just walk until my burden feels lifted. At other times, I have spontaneous images or insights. Sometimes I just sleep. I look forward to this morning alone in nature and guard the time as sacrosanct. As the weeks and months roll on, I can feel my relationship with nature deepen and my sense of alienation lessen.

Recently, I experienced what I think of as an initiation into the path of nature as spiritual journey. Jeanne and I spent ten days at a wilderness retreat in the rain forest on the Caribbean island of Dominica. For two nature people who yearn for a simpler life, this was an extraordinary experience. We lived in the midst of gigantic palm, banana, breadfruit, papaya and mango trees with a waterfall about 100 feet from our cottage. Only a half mile hike from our room were two more waterfalls, each one over 200 feet high. The local people call them the "Mama" and "Papa" falls. The image of looking upward as the water cascaded over the mountain ledge onto the rocks below is forever etched in my memory.

The afternoon after my 54th birthday, I was doing my meditation near the smaller falls outside our cottage. It had become my daily ritual to meditate at this spot. Oftentimes there were moments of connection to the soul of the falls, a sense of kinship with this fellow creature. In my imagery the upper falls - "Mama" and "Papa" - had parented this lower falls. We were brothers. This particular afternoon, I brought my bathing suit with me. After my usual meditation I put it on and mindfully entered the pool at the foot of the falls. I knew that something special was happening, if I continued to follow my intuition, but I had no idea what it was. My impulse was to immerse my entire body in the rushing water but the power of the falls was so great, greater than I, that it stopped me. Instead I stood as close as I could, in the milky foam of the pool, and, closing my eyes, felt the spray of the falls over my body. I imagined myself fully immersed, imagined myself being baptized. The image of the "Mama" and "Papa" falls came into my mind, flowing into the "child" falls, flowing over me, "nature's child."

As I reflected on this experience later, I felt that, by following my intuition and the beckoning of nature, my deeper Self and nature had come together to create a ritual of initiation for me. It was then that I felt fully and firmly the rightness of nature as my spiritual path. I was powerfully struck, too, that this baptism had occurred at the start of my 55th year.

Traditionally, baptisms or initiations require that the initiate take on a new name. When I related my experience at the falls to Jeanne, she teasingly named me "Socratrees" because of my love for trees and my desire to bring to others the wisdom of the woods. The name is just right for me and yet the playfulness of it keeps me from getting carried away with the idea of being a nature mystic! My experience by the falls that April day also captures for me a gradual sense of remembering something lost, something long ago. As I allow myself to go more freely into nature, I feel as if I am returning to an ancestral home. It is as if the collective memory of my Irish heritage is emerging from deep within me. Before the madness of modern culture and the rise of the Christian church, I was an Irish man, a pagan, a man of the woods and the countryside. Nature was my original path. Since my ritual at the falls, that ancestral memory is even stronger. I feel a sense of rightness, serenity, remembering and at-homeness.

Over 100 years ago, Emerson wrote, "Foregoing generations beheld God and nature face to face; we through their eyes. Why should we not also enjoy an original relation to the universe?...and a religion of revelation to us . . . "[32] These words are even more poignant for our times, when the sense of alienation from God and creation (nature) has increased exponentially. Emerson was recommending that we have personal, direct experience of God, to experience the One by connecting with nature "face-to-face." The face of God, however, is not always benevolent. Nor is the face of nature. While often my Thursday morning sojourns are times of peaceful reverie, I have also spent my share of time in a spiritual "no man's land" – the image of the desert seems quite apt. Periods of dryness are inevitable, in fact, necessary on our spiritual journey. This is the time when all feels lost; when we no longer know what we have previously known; when we are sure there is no end to this darkness, that no light will ever shine forth. And then, by some miracle, by some process that is not in our control, we emerge from this desolate place. Just as day always, without fail, follows night, and the cold, frozen desolation of winter is inevitably followed by the blossoming that comes with spring, we find that what we thought we knew has fallen away and new buds of knowing have been gestating. And suddenly we are alive again.

These images of light and dark abound in nature and mirror both the joyful and desolate times in our spiritual journey. Mostly we want to experience the joyful and creative times and we try to avoid the dark and desolate times. But to do so leaves us less than whole. As a guide on our spiritual journey, nature teaches us to learn from and move through the dark times into the light.

As a spiritual path, nature also teaches us that we are all part of a whole. We are interconnected, fellow creatures of the larger Creation, at once separate and part of something greater. While we may believe this as part of our religious or philosophical systems, most of us do not really "know" it in an experiential, heart- and soul-felt way. If we really knew this interconnection, we would relate to other people, the animals, birds, rivers and plants in a different way. In the Native American way, nature is a "community of living beings," of trees, animals, plants, rivers, etc., that are interrelated in this way: "With all beings and all things we shall be as relatives."[33] At the end of the sacred pipe ceremony, the Lakota Sioux cry out, "We are all related," thus acknowledging the mysterious connection of all that contains the "breath of the Great Spirit." And again, Buddha's injunction: "know ye the grasses and the trees . . . " By spending regular, conscious time in nature, we can begin to feel the connecting web that underlies all things.

Another of nature's teachings is about the presence of God or the Divine. As a boy, I was taught that "God is everywhere." Rather than feeling reassured by those words, I developed an image of God as this bearded old man with big eyes and a large notebook. He could see everything I did and was making notations about my infractions for Judgment Day. This was a frightening image of a ubiquitous, powerful, punitive God. It created distance rather than closeness between us. Much time and many different experiences of God since then have helped to change this image. This Native American chant captures quite closely my current experience of God:

O Great Spirit
Earth, wind, sky and sea
You are inside
And all around me.[34]

As I allow myself to contemplate the meaning of this chant and to know it in the center of my being, a different relationship with God and creation emerges and evolves. "God is everywhere" begins to mean that the divine spark exists in all of us creatures. To begin to connect to that produces moments of communion, of nonduality. Of course, this requires an unlearning or letting go of my traditional Judeo-Christian beliefs. I was taught that humans are separate from, superior to and more important than the other creatures. We are the "chosen people." Most religions present some version of this theme, that those of us who belong to a particular church or sect are superior to those who don't (the nonbelievers). The nonbelievers are excluded until they begin to believe. If other people are excluded, where do the other creatures fit in the hierarchy? Either outside or in some lower echelon. While this is traditional Judeo-Christian teaching, there has always been a concurrent, but hidden mystical message of interconnection and oneness with the other creatures. In the Book of Job, God says, "But ask the beasts and they will teach you; the birds of the sky, they will teach you; or speak to the earth, it will teach you; the fish of the sea, they will inform you . . . "[35] St. Francis wrote in the "Canticle of the Sun" of "Brother Sun," "Sister Moon and the Stars," "Brother Wind," "Sister Water," "Brother Fire" and "our Sister, Mother Earth."[36] We need to rediscover the truth of these and other early teachings and integrate them in a meaningful way into our complex, modern world.

How do we begin to develop a more inclusive spirituality? One step is to consider the multiple planes of existence. On the physical plane, we have a particular physical form. The other creatures have different physical forms: wolf, ant, hemlock, rock. On the psychological plan we have personalities and human consciousness. The other creatures have different ways of being in the world and different kinds of consciousness: crowness, oakness, dolphinness. On the spiritual plane there is just Spirit, the anima mundi, the One, the Divine within:

> O Great Spirit
> Earth, wind, sky and sea
> You are inside
> And all around me.[34]

As we spend time in nature, we can begin to look at the other creatures and see their particular form and recognize that it is different from ours. We can see their way of being in the world and recognize that it is different from ours. These differences keep us separate. But then we can begin to contemplate that somewhere within that form and within that personality there is Spirit. Ram Dass has a beautiful and heartwarming way of bridging this separation and connecting to the essence of the other. When we meet another person (or creature), he says, we need to look beyond their individual form and beyond their particular role or personality and say, "Hello in there!"[37] We might continue, "That's an interesting form you have, and you have fascinating (disgusting) ways of being in the world, but underneath those we are brothers and sisters. Hello in there!" These are magical moments of communion. Barriers between us fall down, however briefly, and we connect

172

as fellow creatures of the Great Spirit. Hello in there!

On my walks in the woods there are these precious moments when a fox walks on the path and we stop and look at each other for a while, suspended in time, connected to each other. At these times, I feel a sense of love and union; a smile comes to my face and I say, "Hi, little one!" At other times a certain tree has an aura of invitation surrounding it. We connect at the level of spiritual family and the words "big brother" come from within. Or I touch a leaf or feel a rock or smell a flower and say "Hello in there!" A chipmunk runs quickly across my path and I say unselfconsciously, "Hi, friend." A crow's caw startles me from my preoccupation and I say "Thanks for stopping by, brother." These are brief moments of dropping barriers of Self and physical form, of belief system and role to allow a connection, spirit-to-spirit. It is a recognition that "Spirit" is everywhere, hidden by form. The spark of the divine is everywhere. God is everywhere. I have discovered a way of extending these moments. If I stop whatever I am doing and be consciously loving, the moment of communion seems to be extended and suspended in time. "Hello in there. There is no need to be afraid of me. We are fellow creatures of the woods. I love you as a brother and a friend." I stand or sit there without moving, saying to myself "let go of fear" and continue to send that message of love. The precious moments of nonduality, of nonalienation are increasing. Our friendship is deepening.

This path of nature of which I speak, is not a nature-based religion with a belief system in which nature is deified or "nature spirits" are divinities. In my exploration, I am attempting to return to the mystical roots of spiritual practice, to spend time in nature consciously, as a meditative act, with the intent of going beyond the form of human, animal or plant to connect with all Creation spirit to spirit.

My friend, Jim Carney, who is also on a path to God through nature, recently sent me a poem he wrote more than 20 years ago. This poem captures for me the essential, intuitive knowing we all have, however deeply buried, that we are not alone, that Spirit connects us all, and that God, in whatever form, is everywhere.

## Alone?

Overcast sky, drizzle, wind from the northwest, Noisy surf - ingredients for a solitary stroll - on a deserted Lake Michigan shoreline.

Wet footprints trail behind. It's cool, jacket weather, but warm inside. A glow. Is it the Spirit that speaks there? Bringing peace. Silently. Without words.

Surf washes the sandy shore; all ahead - to forever; and behind. Loudly. Rhythmically. In tune with the wind; and the earth - and me (and He?).

A seagull sits on the wind above; a sculptured, arresting stillness; playing on the thermals. Motionless – drifting sideways – moving past slowly, like time; then gone. – A memory of grace.

Off to the side, near the empty wooded dunes, a mystery: a single post. Wet. Alone. Surrounded only by the wild beach grasses. Put there by whom? And why? And where is he?

An old stump – driftwood – roots reaching out like gnarled, arthritic fingers. – A thing of beauty. – Designed by a master craftsman. – And polished by His sand.

Wet footprints trail behind. It's cool, jacket weather, but warm inside. A glow. Is it the Spirit that speaks there? Bringing peace. Silently. Without words.[38]

# DARKNESS

So far we have been talking about the benevolent side of nature; her beauty and bounty; her capacity for nurturing and healing. But what about the dark side of nature? What about her capacity for destruction; her power to destroy a whole town or village in a matter of minutes by a tornado or to slowly wipe out hundreds of square miles of homes and farms through flooding? What about the devastation by fire to Yellowstone and the Long Island Pine Barrens in the early 1990s? What do we say about the relationship of predator and prey; the wolf who knows instinctively the weak or sickly caribou in the herd? What might nature teach us about our own "shadow" by looking at her dark side?

---

Darkness takes different forms. In the dark, the mood of our home changes. Rooms "feel" different in the dark. Jungian analyst John Sanford says that our minds are different in the darkness. We see things in the darkness that we don't see in the light. Our friend, Marta, told us a story of what she saw in the dark. When her son, Jake, was little, she went up to his room to check on him one night. When she walked into the room, she saw an apparition of an old woman bending over Jake in his bed. "Go back where you came from," she told the old woman, "you don't belong here." The apparition drifted across the room and then was gone. Who can really say with certainty where this night-form came from, but it is unlikely that the same scene would have unfolded had it been daylight. What does this say about the nature of the night and is impact on us? What does it say about the dark side of our personalities?

Carl Jung, the Swiss psychoanalyst, wrote extensively on the "shadow" aspects or the "dark side" of the personality. He considered all of the contents of the unconscious to be shadow aspects of Self. We harbor all kinds of unwanted or unacceptable creatures in the shadows of our inner world: the angry man, the sensuous woman, the frightened child, the fool. All those aspects of Self that have gone wanting for lack of affection or affirmation, whose existence we'd prefer not to know about; the parts of Self we consider "negative" and so deny. But, by denying them we lose access to many of the jewels that exist as part of a more complete, or whole, personality. Other forms, rich, creative aspects of Self, also lurk in the dark corners of the psyche: the artist, the philosopher, the athlete, the writer, the intellectual, the entrepreneur. Frequently, negative shadow figures stand blocking the creative shadow aspects of Self. Unexpressed anger prevents us from activating the energy needed to write. Fear of our sexuality blocks creative energy that might go into a painting or sculpture. Acknowledging or releasing the negative aspects of our shadow can act to energize our creative

Self. So trained are we, however, to believe that certain parts of us will be destructive to others or ourselves that we ignore or deny their existence. To do so leaves us less than whole. Some time after the fires in Yellowstone and the Long Island Pine Barrens, naturalists found that the seeds of certain pines could only have been released through the intense heat of these devastating brush fires. Their occurrence is not only natural, but necessary to the growth of this particular species of trees. In the same way, we lose out on possible growth that can emerge from exploring and experiencing the fire and turbulence of our own darkness.

##  Bill

As a boy and a young man, I was full of anger. I did not express it, but acted it out mainly by setting small fires in the woods by my home. I remember the storms of anger displayed by many of the adults in my life. I felt the ravagings of those storms and this left me fearful of my own seemingly uncontrollable affective storms of rage. Because anger was not expressed in healthy ways in my family, I saw only its destructive side. Not wanting to leave a trail of destruction and fearing that, once begun, these storms of emotion would never end, until recent years I denied or controlled them. I was also given another powerful message about anger and aggression as a boy. I was quite tall from a very young age and my mother frequently expressed to me her fear that I would hurt someone because of my size. "You're so big," she would tell me, "you have to be careful not to hurt anyone." Desiring her love and approval I learned to suppress anger and aggression for fear of hurting others. Her fear became my fear. As an adult, I worked through a lot of this early issue in psychotherapy. But in recent years, my interest in wolves and my conscious identification with the wolf have helped me get to a deeper level of acceptance of this shadow aspect of myself. If we do not become conscious of our shadow, it will act in unconscious, destructive ways or we will project the qualities of our shadow onto others. Then, we do not see the anger in ourselves, but in everyone around us.

Actively using the image of the wolf – imagining myself as a wolf stalking my prey; feeling myself in the sleek, strong body of a wolf; imagining a wolf walking alongside me as a protector – has helped me to better identify anger at the moment I am feeling it, rather than suppressing it and having it slip out later in some unconscious way. The "inner wolf" helps me to sense physical as well as emotional danger. If someone tries to hurt or humiliate me or someone I love, I feel a fierce growl that comes from some deep place inside me. This inner growl sometimes gets expressed in a warning burst of anger. At other times, it gets channeled into an act of self-assertion. I have used this animal sound to frighten off aggressive dogs. And once, when Jeanne and I were sitting on a large rock in the middle of a field at night, my wolf-growl caused an approaching coyote to retreat. As an aspect of accepting my own darkness, I like this power that can frighten other animals.

Over the years I have acquired several books about wolves that have taught me about their behavior. I have studied them so that I can understand and integrate the many aspects of the wolf nature. Wolves do not kill indiscriminately, but only out of necessity. In the same way, I need to express anger or aggression when a situation calls for it and not unleash old rage toward those who don't deserve it. I also identify with the other images of the wolf: the stamina and perseverance, the loyalty to the pack, and, paradoxically perhaps, the image of the lone wolf. Allowing myself to experience my own "wolf nature" in all of its aspects generates feelings of deeper connectedness to myself, nature and the animal world.

When I think about the dark side of my own psyche and the darkness of nature, storms, too, come to mind. I love walking outside in a blizzard, or in the eye of a hurricane, or watching a pyrotechnic lightening display from a safe perch outside. I am awed by this immense power of nature, so much greater than mine. At the same time, it connects me to my own power and my fear of its potential to destroy. We tend to judge our emotions, especially anger, as bad, weak or sinful. By contrast, in nature there is no judgment. We do not say that nature is bad, weak or sinful. The destruction that is left may be bad, but nature is just being nature. Storms come, they run their course and they pass. Of course, in our human emotional storms, we cannot blindly rage and leave a path of destruction wherever we go. This generally happens, however, only when normal anger is continually denied and can no longer be suppressed, or when we have unresolved issues of anger. In the course of expressing our feelings we do sometimes cause hurt, pain or damage. But just as nature slowly comes back to life after a storm, flood or fire and the landscape is transformed, we also can mend, heal and be transformed by the pain in our relationships.

The story of Frank, a strong, stocky young man in his late twenties, illustrates how such anger can develop, the destruction it causes and how nature – the ocean in this case – can help in healing the wounds of this anger.

Frank has large hands and Popeye-like forearms. He came to therapy because of his problems controlling his anger. He had been arrested for DWIs several times and had spent some time in jail on assault charges. "I have never hit a woman, though," Frank explains, because that goes against his moral code. But he has lost several girlfriends because they have become frightened or "fed up with my temper." It is humiliating for Frank to admit that his life is out of control and that he needs help.

Not surprisingly, Frank's father is an alcoholic who had problems controlling his temper. He is a carpenter who rides a motorcycle to work and proudly sports several tattoos. Frequently, he beat Frank with his fists, knocking his head against the wall and strapping him with his belt. He was an unrelenting storm of rage. As Frank developed physically in his mid-teens, he became bigger and stronger than his father. When he was 15 years old, his father stormed after him brandishing his fists, ready to strike again. Instead of cowering as usual to protect himself from the blows, Frank turned, pointed his finger at his father's face and, fueled by the "rage of a lifetime" said, "Come on. If you touch me I'll kill you." Frank meant it. And his father knew he meant it and was physically capable of doing it. That afternoon the beatings ended. Still, periodically his father would erupt and walk toward Frank ready to strike. Each time Frank would invite his father to "just try and hit me!" and then warn him, "Touch me and you're a dead man!" His father recognized the truth of that warning and backed down each time.

Frank had vivid memories of those beatings and how terrified he was for so many years. "No one will ever make me feel like that again. No one will ever hurt me again. If anyone tries to, I go nuts and beat the shit out of them." As he talks, the pain, terror, humiliation and resultant murderous rage are simultaneously present.

Clearly Frank's hypervigilance and readiness to explode are directly related to his relationship with his father. But Frank's relationship with his mother also contributed to his explosions of anger. Frank's mother was self-absorbed, complaining unceasingly to him about how hard her life was with his father. She was emotionally cold and hardened, supplying him with little of the maternal nourishment he needed. She lavished praise upon Frank's two younger sisters, but to him her repeated refrain was "You're just like your father!" Since it was no secret how much she hated Frank's father, that phrase had a poisonous impact on Frank's self-worth and fueled his rage.

Frank loves the sea. Whether he is sailing a simple Sunfish, digging for clams to make some extra money, fishing with his friends or camping overnight at the beach, he feels happiest and calmest when he is near or in the water. He recalls that the best time of his life was in his early twenties when he was playing drums in a rock bank at night and deep sea diving during the day. "The diving was so relaxing. I just loved being underwater. It made me feel so centered. I didn't have any problems with my temper the whole time I was diving." As the therapy progressed and Frank released some of his anger toward his parents, I talked with him about the symbolism of the sea, the mythological and linguistic references to the sea as feminine; the connection to the amniotic fluid of the womb; the primordial connections to the collective unconscious, to his anima or soul aspect. Each of these meanings resonated with Frank at different levels. He began to understand in a conscious way what he already "knew" unconsciously; that to be in or near the sea was a source of mothering for him. He was seeking maternal nourishment that he never received; he was seeking refuge from the rage of his father; he was trying to integrate his own deep feminine; he was seeking, as Robert Bly describes, the "male mother"[39] that his father was unable to be. As Frank became more aware of the meaning of the sea in his life, he began to seek it out in a more conscious way for his healing and to develop a relationship with the sea as Divine Mother. He stopped sailing competitively and would just sail solo whenever he felt troubled. He took his guitar to the beach and poems and songs began to emerge. He started taking herbal baths at night and his long-term insomnia began to lift. His storms of rage came much less often and lasted for shorter periods of time. Unfortunately Frank ended his therapy before he had fully worked through his old anger. He decided to move away from his parents and live on the California coast. Hopefully he will continue this work down the road and for now carry with him the powerful image of the sea, spending time there to help him heal.

⁂

In nature there are predators and there is prey. In fact, one day the owl preys on the squirrel and the next day the coyote preys on the owl. So the owl is both predator and prey. This is the nature of the animal world. We are not so different. Frank's father is a predator. He was likely prey to his own father. Frank was his prey. And for a while Frank was a predator. In the animal realm, this dynamic is a natural and necessary means of survival. In the human realm, if acted out unconsciously, this predator-prey dynamic serves only to destroy our sense of Self and our relationships with others. For instance, a young girl who was abused by her father often grows into a woman who is constantly the victim of abusive men. In adulthood, she is unconsciously acting out the role of "prey." She, in turn, is likely to prey on others, often her children, unconsciously acting out the role of "predator." This does not have to be in the form of physical abuse or extreme emotional abuse, but often takes the more subtle forms of hypercriticalness, overprotectiveness or controlling behavior. In those instances, the prey is the child's inner Self. Internally, the mother's sense of Self is almost nonexistent. Externally, her relationships continue to reflect the predator/prey dynamic – she, acting out both roles in different relationships – and her life brings her little joy. If, however, the woman can become aware of this continuing dynamic in her life, she can consciously activate the inner predator as a protector, thus freeing herself from a lifelong pattern of abuse.

## 🐾 Jeanne

In my work as a therapist I see many women who are victims of abuse. The abuse runs the gamut, from hypercritical, judgmental mothers who keep their daughters connected to them through subtle forms of emotional blackmail, to fathers who raped or otherwise molested them as young girls. Of course, some version of these abusive relationships is repeated in adulthood with a husband or other life partner and in friendships. The work with these women is long and arduous because of the deep and often devastating impact of the early family relationships, but also because our culture still fosters a subservient and submissive view of women. With all the social, political, and psychological work that has been done in the last 30 years, we still have much to do to free ourselves of the long-held belief that women should be submissive to any authority but their own.

While my own background was emotionally deficient rather than abusive, I did not escape the messages that women commonly receive from family and culture. I learned that I must defer to men because they are more intelligent; that I am here to take care of the emotional needs of others - my own needs are not of value; that anger, especially, is forbidden; that sexuality is bad - I should not live fully in my body; that men are only interested in me for sex. Needless to say, I was in a submissive role in most of my adult relationships, male and female, until I went into therapy and began to work through these early issues.

During that time, I became very interested in mythology, imagery and symbolism. I was fascinated with Carl Jung's work on the archetypal images that emerge from the collective psyche of a culture and the personal symbols that give meaning to our experiences. I also began training as a social worker and psychotherapist at the Psychosynthesis Institute of New York. Psychosynthesis is a psychological framework based on the little-known work of Roberto Assagioli. Assagioli was an Italian psychiatrist who developed his own theories about the human psyche at the same time as Freud and Jung. While he incorporated some of the work of his colleagues, Assagioli brought an extra dimension to his own work that is particularly relevant to today's psychotherapeutic culture. Assagioli studied a broad range of mystical and spiritual traditions from Christian mysticism to Zen Buddhism. While he himself was a spiritual man, he was also a pragmatist who found ways to integrate some of the disciplines and philosophies of these systems as tools in his psychological model. Like Jung, Assagioli also believed deeply in the power of our intrapsychic images to affect the circumstances of our lives. He developed practical ways for people to actively use these images for their psychological and spiritual growth. Using Assagioli's "guided imagery" techniques helped to me access many of my own shadow parts. These "subpersonalities" acted unconsciously to wreak havoc with my relationships and my inner life. As Assagioli suggested, I gave names to these different parts of myself and experienced their inner presence powerfully through the images of my mind's eye.[40]

For me imagery is very visual. I can close my eyes and have vivid, detailed pictures come to me. But not everyone has visual images. For some people, imagery comes through the other senses. Some people "hear" images; other people "feel" images in their bodies; some people "taste" or "smell" images, while others may have "thought forms" that come into their minds. Each of these is a way of experiencing our own unique and distinctive internal imagery.

The very first time I used Assagioli's imaging technique, I imagined myself climbing a mountain and entering a "temple of silence" that stood at the top of the mountain. Inside all was silence and I stood in a beam of sunlight that poured in from an opening at the peak of the temple. Then I went to meet another aspect of my personality. The woman who approached me was a mirror image of myself, dressed in jeans and a sweatshirt. But she was so obviously completely comfortable with herself. She was earthy and sensual, fully alive in her body, and at the same time, I sensed, connected to something deeply spiritual. This shadow aspect of myself frightened me. When I first saw her, I thought she was "the seductress" but she told me she was my "Earth Mother." She told me not to be afraid of her and that "if we give love without expectations it will be returned to us a hundredfold."

At the time I could grasp little of the significance of this image or the true meaning of her words. Fifteen years later, I have acquired some deeper understanding of her origins. A core dynamic in my psychology has been a split between body and spirit. This has its roots in a strict Christian environment, at home and in school, that maintained that all desires of the body were basically evil. And yet, my body was full of desires of all kinds. But they got stuffed into that "long, black bag" in which we hide our shadow. How could I be a spiritual woman, which I also desired intensely, and live in this body with its many wants and needs? Even my birth sign, Sagittarius, the Centaur, epitomized this core issue – half man, half animal – spirit and matter joined together. Over years of working through this very difficult struggle, I came to see that my Earth Mother symbolized the resolution of this split. She was a projection of possibility, an image of a future Self. She was my earthy, grounded, intuitive, sensual Self. A Self in which body and spirit are synthesized, in which to be spiritual means to live fully in my body. And that to love from that place of wholeness is to give fully of my own substantiveness, not from a place of emptiness. If I love from my own fullness, then the love I receive in return is extra.

After meeting my Earth Mother, over years other subpersonalities came into my imagery. Hannah was "the vile old beggar woman," stooped over in her ragged, dirty clothes, worthy enough only to sweep the streets behind others. She was the image of all my suppressed emotional neediness, a part of myself that I particularly disliked and refused for a long time to even acknowledge. When I finally did recognize Hannah and began to accept her, her whole presence in my imagery changed. She stood up straight and wore different clothes and no longer was left to sweep up after others. Concurrently, I was better able to acknowledge my own needs, accept them and express them.

Sam, dressed as a court jester was another sub personality. He was "the Fool." Silly, lazy and idle, Sam loved to play and always walked hand in hand with a little girl. But in my images, Sam was sad because he was a prisoner. All he wanted was to be set free to play with the little girl at his side. Later on, I met my "Wise Old Man" in my imagery. He was the archetypal image of my deep Self, my soul, the part of me that knows just exactly what I need for my Self from moment to moment.

Working with each of these shadow images was a profoundly rich experience for me and helped me to synthesize these various aspects of a more complete, more complex Self. Once they were released from "the darkness" into consciousness, they no longer had the power to work on me unconsciously. And, while much had been synthesized through this imagery work, I still had difficulty asserting myself and expressing anger directly. As I continued to work through the early issues that made this difficult for me, I also used the imagery and my observations of nature as tools to help me express my anger. My underlying fear was that, if I expressed anger, I would be subjected to the anger of the other in return and, ultimately, be rejected. What I needed was to feel protected; that if the other was angry, it would not harm me and if I were rejected, well then, that would be okay, too. I would be okay. I also needed to feel a sense of my own power to strongly and firmly express my feelings of anger.

While walking in the fields one day and mulling this over, an image spontaneously came into my mind of a panther. She was sleek, black and obviously powerful. I knew immediately that she was an ally and imagined her walking beside me. As the image came more vividly into my mind's eye, I could feel in my body the dynamic, protective power of the panther. My body straightened and firmed; I held my head a bit higher. The panther was my protector; her power became mine. Over time, I allowed this image to come into my mind frequently. As I felt more of the panther's power, I began to assert myself more fully, imagining the panther circling protectively around me. I knew that if I needed to attack I could, and that my own "panther energy" would keep me from harm. Paradoxically, when we connect with our anger or aggression consciously, we rarely need to attack unless we are in physical danger. Otherwise we need only, in the end, protect ourselves from emotional and psychological violence.

It is important to trust images that come to us spontaneously. The deeper Self knows what we need and, when we are still and receptive, provides us with images to aid us on our journey. It is striking to me how often the image of a large cat, like my panther, comes into the dreams or images of women I work with. That these animal images come to us spontaneously says something powerful about our unconscious connection to nature. Nurturing them, fostering them, going out into nature in order to deepen that connection aids in strengthening these images as our psychic protectors.

In working with women and young girls, I will often use imagery with animals or spontaneous images from the natural world to work on issues of physical and emotional safety and personal empowerment.

Julie was twelve when she started therapy. She was shy and fearful and intimidated daily by the "tough kids" in her junior high school. Julie is quite bright and had mature insights into the deeper source of her fears. She vividly recalled the times before her parents were divorced when her father would come home from the bar and violently attack her mother. Always fearful that her father's anger would be turned against her, Julie became a "good kid," agreeable and complacent. These insights, however, were insufficient. She needed something more to consciously activate the dormant or underdeveloped assertive part of her personality. Using guided imagery, I had Julie close her eyes, focus on her breath for a few minutes, and then imagine herself walking down a path through the woods, noticing all the while what was around her. What kind of day was it? How did the ground feel beneath her feet? Did she hear sounds? What smells came by on the breeze? After a little while, she came to a circular clearing in the woods where, I told her, she would see an animal that would act as her protector. Julie immediately imagined a large tiger standing in the field and named her Crystal. We took several minutes for her to feel the strength and protective energy of her tiger, to imagine taking that power inside herself as she breathed in deeply. Julie worked diligently and quickly with the image of the "Crystal Tiger Power." She drew pictures of her and imagined her at night before going to sleep and on waking each morning. I encouraged Julie to learn more about tigers, to read books or watch TV shows about the tiger. In a short time the imagery helped Julie begin to integrate this shadow aspect of herself into consciousness. She showed greater self-assurance and carried herself with more confidence. She began to assert herself more in general, at home and at school, and her difficulties with the tough kids lessened significantly.

<hr />

While my panther and Julie's tiger came to each of us spontaneously as inner protector animals, the "big cats" in Ellie's imagery that follows are not, at first, benevolent figures. In fact, they emerge from the darkness, from the shadow, to guide Ellie more deeply into her Self.

Ellie was in her mid-thirties and had been in therapy on and off for several years. While she had worked through many layers of her core psychological issues, she still struggled with her image of herself as a woman. In her fundamentalist Christian family, the body was all but denied; pleasure, especially physical pleasure, was forbidden. Expressing the life of the mind and the Spirit was the valued way of being in Ellie's family. The phrase she used to describe her family's attitude toward the body was, "If it feels good, don't do it." Ellie had followed the family dictum most of her life, and yet she longed for a loving relationship in which she could experience herself fully as a sexual woman. The imagery she experienced one early spring day marked a shift for Ellie in this inner struggle.

> It is cloudy and misting this morning when I wake; still kind of dark outside. I lie in bed and hear the birds singing. It is beautiful. I have the uncanny sense that I am in a stone cottage in the English countryside. Lots of vines and flowers are ready to bloom in the gardens out front. I walk out of the cottage and down to the edge of the road. To my left is the village; to my right, open countryside and a forest in the distance. Though I want to go to the village, something is pulling me to go to the right. I walk down the road, past the open fields and enter the woods. The trees seem very tall. The path leads to a circular clearing; I am aware that it is the place of a god and goddess. As sunlight streams into the clearing, I know that an offering must be made. I lie down on a stone slab within the circle. The sunlight shines on me and disintegrates my clothing. I lie naked. A man comes towards me. He is the man of the forest. He lays me on the grass and we make love. He is strong and powerful, but tender. When we are finished, he dresses me in a simple, white Grecian dress. Then he gives me a golden staff. I know it will protect me.

I continue on the path until I come to a cave. I know there are jungle animals inside and that I am protected by the golden staff, but still I am afraid to go in. Finally I enter. It is like a tunnel, very large, very dark. The animals are very large, too, and although they are embedded in the walls, they can reach me with their claws. They are clawing at me, ripping my clothing and skin, flinging me from side to side. Though I am frightened and my skin is open with wounds, I have no sensation of pain. The animals are all large cats: lions, panthers, leopards, tigers. As I enter the second half of the cave, there are more of these same animals, but these cats are licking my wounds. I begin to see light at the opening at the other end of the cave and an old, gray-haired woman waiting for me.

When I come out of the tunnel, it is light, not sunlight, just a lightness within the forest. The old woman leads me up a path more deeply into the forest to her home in the base of a giant tree, like a redwood. A soft, golden light glows inside the tree. The old woman lays me down on a bed of straw and bathes my wounds. As they begin to heal, she speaks to me. She tells me I am very courageous to go through the cave; most women don't make it that far. I am tired and feel a longing within me. I tell her I ache to be loved fully as a woman. She tells me I am still a child in matters of love and that I am going through the trials. I ask what it means that I am still a child in matters of love. She says there needs to be more deepening; that is when love blooms most fully, when there is deepening. As she speaks, I have the sensation of a very large flower blossoming within my whole chest. She tells me to rest; now is my time to be nurtured and cared for. She will care for me. I feel it is safe for me to do that. I know the old woman is a shaman.

A number of archetypal images are woven through Ellie's imagery. The image of initiation or rebirth: entering the cave or tunnel, enduring the "trials," and emerging, as from the birth canal, into the light. The image of the "temenos," a Greek work that refers to a sacred enclosure in nature that is dedicated to a god or goddess, also has an archetypal feel to it. Jung used the term temenos to capture the image of an inner space where the Self can develop and be nurtured. Surely this is exactly what is unfolding in Ellie's imagery, a deeper understanding of her Self.

Another archetypal image is that of the "hieros gamos" or sacred marriage. Ellie "knows" that an offering must be made and that she will make love with the "man of the forest." She needs, as every woman does, to submit herself, not to the man, but to the "god of instinct." Only by awakening to the slumbering desire within can a woman become fully herself. Through the ritual act of offering herself to the "man of the forest," Ellie is invited to take full responsibility for her instinctual life. Only then can she truly enter into love that emerges from personal relatedness.

The cats, too, refer to the instinctual life. In Jungian terms, they are connected to the instinctual power of the deep feminine. Because her mother had suppressed her own sensuality and sexuality, Ellie had great difficulty in accepting herself as a sexual woman. Stirrings of any sensual pleasure were rare and feelings of sexual attractiveness or desire were followed by feelings of guilt and self-loathing. The shadow aspect of her mother's "cat" had left Ellie terribly wounded.

But what wounds us also has the power to heal us, just as the cats that clawed at Ellie then licked her wounds. This imagery guided Ellie more deeply into herself, to explore her sexuality and deep feminine and to begin to define herself as a woman separate from her mother, separate from the expectations of men and separate from the images of women in our culture.

Images are powerful. They are symbols that act on us consciously and unconsciously, as Jung said, transforming our psychic energy. In his writings on Psychosynthesis, Assagioli lists seven hierarchical categories of symbols. The first two are nature and animal symbols. This is indicative of their intrapsychic power, their ability to set into motion synthesizing psychological processes. Images from nature enable us to accept those unloved parts of ourselves that we now judgmentally label as "dark." This synthesis of previously unwanted aspects of our personality will result in a sense of greater inner peace and freedom.

My gifted friend, Sally, is a kinesthetic psychic and healer. She uses her ability to "read" body energies to help me process information and experiences on different levels of consciousness. Sometimes we are silent while she works and the processing goes on at a cellular level. Sometimes she talks with me about what she is sensing. One winter day in 1995 as she worked over me, Sally told me that she kept seeing an image of me in a dark, primordial forest carrying a candle in my hand. Fascinated by the image, we talked for a while about what it might mean. Was its message a literal one? Was I to go into the forest at night bearing a candle? Or was the message to be taken symbolically as, say, the need to bring light to the darkness? Did I need to be aware of something I was not? We speculated about each of these together and I continued to ponder the image alone for a couple of weeks afterward. I was struggling at the time to know more fully the complexity of myself as a woman. I do not want to be limited by inaccurate, external paradigms of "womanness" and so what comes up from the dark of the unconscious is especially important to me. Trusting Sally's gift of tapping into other ways of "knowing," I wondered why this image was coming up now.

Before the times of the witch burnings, women would often go into the woods at night and sit in circles around a sacred fire, dance and perform rituals of healing. They must have felt comfortable in the dark to do that. These were European women, the medicine women and healers in their small villages and in the countryside. These women, my ancestors, were connected to their feminine power – the power of healing, the power of sexuality, the power of intuition and deep knowing. As Donna Reed depicts in her documentary, "The Burning Times," these strong women were threatening to the men of the cities, the men of the Church, the wealthy men of the Industrial Revolution. This was an incredibly dark time in our history as women.[41]

As I continued to ponder Sally's image, I wondered whether or not I could go into the woods alone at night. The idea of it both frightened and excited me. Even if the image was symbolic, perhaps a ritual enactment of it would shift something for me intra-psychically. I debated and suggested to Sally that maybe I could go if Bill were somewhere close by. But she said that, no, I was definitely by myself in this image. No one else was around.

A few weeks later, on an unusually mild Sunday night in December, I decided spontaneously to do it. Bill was away for the weekend and my sons were out for the evening. I would go into the woods alone and just see what happened. I took a candle, matches, a pad of paper and a pen and stuck them in my Guatemalan bag, thrust the bag over my shoulder and walked off in the dark toward the woods. I had been there just that morning to spend some time in meditation. I wondered how different it would feel now, in the dark. Very quickly, I managed to get off the path and found myself entangled in some bushes. Just as quickly, I made my way back to the trail. I did not have to go very far before I felt myself in the grip of all my own fears of darkness. "Who might be in these woods to cause me harm? Was someone following me from the road? Would I meet some terrifying creature?" Ridiculous questions in light of day, but in the dark . . . Further in, where the path opens up to a long, straight corridor through the cathedral pines, I lighted my candle. To my surprise, I found that I had more difficulty seeing with the candle lit. I was quite vigilant of my surroundings and the candle created a glare. Perhaps I should have heeded the words of Wendell Berry:

> To go in the dark with a light is to know the light.
> To know the dark, go dark. Go without sight,
> And find that the dark, too, blooms and sings,
> And is traveled by dark feet and dark wings.[42]

But this night I carried my candle tightly in my hand. Shortly, I veered off the path to the left, through some trees, up an easy slope to the tree where I had done my meditation that same morning. A gentle rain began to fall. I heard no sound but the rain and the distant hum of traffic. I placed my candle at the foot of the tree and wondered what I would do next. I had come with no plan, unsure how far into the woods I would even get. I squatted down, the ground was covered with wet leaves. I moved the candle before me and began to pray to the Divine Mother for courage on this journey and help in knowing myself fully as a woman. I was struck by the silence all around me and felt less fearful perched as I was slightly above the path. In between fear-thoughts I wondered why I was doing this. Then I took out my pad and paper and began writing in the dark. The candle did not help me to see and so I blindly scribbled thoughts, feelings and images that came into my mind. Pondering, praying, writing, I stayed a while longer, all the time aware of my fear and my vigilance. I blew out the candle and walked back down to the path. Unexpectedly, I felt even more fearful leaving the woods than I had coming in. I realized later on that, coming in, I knew what was behind me. Leaving, the depth of the woods I had not traveled was at my back. As I neared the edge of the woods, I could already feel an internal sense of courage. I did it! I went into the darkness of the woods all alone with only myself to protect me. My steps felt lighter, in fact, I think perhaps I walked just above the ground!

The following day I shaped what I had written in the woods the night before into a poem:

Step by darkened step
I enter this
primeval wood
wet
as my Mother's womb
with rain-
dank-musky
Earth
rising up to
fill my nostrils

Shadows of
cathedral pine
loom larger than
this morn when
a lifetime ago
I sat in sunlit silence
in this wood
birds and breeze
surrounding me.
Now all is silent
Darkness

but for my candle
lighting your
darkened countenance
so different from
your warm
embracing
daytime face:
heart pounding
shadows
no birds
or wind
just stillness
and
drops of rain.

What struck me most about the woods that night
was how different I felt in the darkness. In the light
of day I felt safe, unthreatened. In the darkness I felt
frightened, vulnerable, hyper-vigilant. The "dark countenance"
of my Mother was a different experience altogether. On the
physical level, of course, I was dealing with diminished visual
sensory and perceptual information created by the lack of
light. Coupled with being alone, this causes anxiety and our
projective processes are set in motion. Experiences we may
have had in the dark, things we have been told about "what
happens in the dark," and psychological fears of facing our
own inner darkness all come into play at different levels of
consciousness. Perhaps, however, there is an additional fear
that is stirred from the collective unconscious: the memory of
what happened to the women who went into the woods at night;
the healers and "shape-changers," or witches; the women who
were the teachers or druids.

After my adventure, another friend told me about an old Celtic ritual that takes place around the time of the winter solstice in which the women would go into the forest at night and light a candle at the base of the largest tree. When I heard this story, I was struck powerfully by the similarity to my own ritual journey, taken intuitively at almost the same time of year and in nearly the same way.

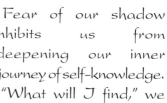

Fear of our shadow inhibits us from deepening our inner journey of self-knowledge. "What will I find," we wonder fearfully, "if I really look inside myself?" Perhaps we each need to walk alone in the woods at night or go on a vision quest or retreat to an isolated cabin by the sea. Or some other symbolic journey into the darkness. Buddha, Jesus, the native Shamans, all spiritual seekers must confront their own inner darkness. We all need to bring light into the darkness - the light of awareness, the warm light of loving acceptance. It is part of becoming whole.

# HOME

## ❧ Bill

One day a few years back, I was taking a walk in one of my favorite nature places. As I crossed an open meadow at the edge of the woods, I was unexpectedly filled with tears. "I want to go home," I said to myself, sobbing. I felt this longing in the totality of my being. It was as if every cell in my body was yearning to go home. I didn't even know what this meant. But for that day, I felt a different sense of connection to all the creatures of the woods. I stopped to touch the leaves, smell the flowers, talk to the chipmunks. I called them "my friend." For a number of hours, I was acutely aware of a profound sense of friendship with everything that I came in contact with. I felt as if the other creatures were extending their hands in friendship or that some barrier had been lifted and that the wall of separation between me and the other creatures had come down. "One touch of nature," Shakespeare wrote, "makes the whole world kin."[43] On this day, I felt that exactly. Nature had touched me. We were experiencing a moment of kinship, a moment of communion. Perhaps I was experiencing something of the sense of original community that existed in the Garden of Eden, my original home.

A long time ago, before our separation from God, we were whole and part of all creation. Somewhere deep within, we remember that state and yearn to return home to it and end our exile. Saint Francis, a nature mystic who was exiled from his biological "familia" but remained connected to all of creation, experienced a deeply personal relationship with God and the other creatures. He spent a lot of time in nature and called the other creations "Brother Sun," "Sister Moon," "Brother Wind" and "Sister Water." All of nature was his kin and recaptured for him, perhaps, a bit of the Garden of Eden. Perhaps, for me on this day, nature had touched my own deeply repressed memory of the original Garden with my original family. The flowers and trees and small creatures and I were all equal in creation. I smiled, laughed, chanted whenever the urge struck. I felt an "unbearable lightness of being." I did not want to leave. Ever. I was home at last.

I did return to the "real world," albeit reluctantly, otherwise I would not be writing this. And, it is here in the real world and in my writing that I try to understand and make sense of and share these periodic moments of powerful connectedness to nature. This is my lifelong journey. When we are touched by nature in this way, we are affected on many different levels. One aspect of this particular experience for me is the spiritual. On this level, I was experiencing directly the pain of separation from God and my rightful place in His/Her presence. With this pain was the longing to bridge the gap and return home. The story of the Garden of Eden is a metaphor for that state of perfect union with God and our subsequent exile from it. To what degree each of us feels this exile and what route we take to find our way back is very individual. But just as the Jews' period of exile ended and they eventually returned to the land of Zion, each individual soul must journey back to the Promised Land, into the presence of God.

Some would say that my desire to enter the woods and never return was a desire to escape. I certainly felt weighted down by the responsibilities, conflicts, small annoyances and alienation of everyday life. To be free of this madness would be wonderful! But there was more happening on that day. I felt not simply a flight from, but a yearning to go toward. Something in me, I'm calling it my soul, wanted to return to some place that it had been before, a place it knew and was remembering, a place of freedom, peace, renewal and connectedness. I call that place home. In my long-term love affair with nature, I have sought out and welcomed any opportunity to be with her. Just as with any lover, there are many levels of our relationship and many motives in the attraction. This experience, however, awakened me to another aspect of my relationship with nature - to bring me closer to God. Now when I enter nature, I approach with a different consciousness. Sometimes. The hardest thing for we humans is to live consciously, to be aware. So now I am aware that there are times when I go into nature to connect with God. I am taking time away from the ordinary world to enter the sacred world. I go to my nature sanctuary or refuge, to a holy place, a place of safety and retreat from the madness of everyday life. This is my Sabbath service. I am attending a private worship service in God's original temple. I have no specific form to this service or specific prayers. Whatever evolves on that particular day is my service. What is essential is the intention in my heart and a prayerful attitude.

Sometimes, I'll be walking and suddenly feel an urge to kneel down. Trying not to feel self-conscious, I kneel. Sometimes, I take this moment to pray for myself, my family, friends or patients. Other times my kneeling is simply a moment of reverence, a mixture of awe at the magnificence of a beam of sunlight shining on a pine bough and a simultaneous sense of being humbled by the power of creation. At other times,

I feel a sense of gratitude to the Creator for creating me and all of this beauty. Sometimes, as I've mentioned before, I start chanting. Initially I felt strange, walking in the woods and feeling the pressure inside of these sounds that wanted to come out of me. Was this the same person who grew up in a tough, working-class housing project (not much chanting going on there!) and who was told at a young age that he was tone deaf and should forget about singing? But the pressure of the sounds was persistent. How could I allow sound to come from me when I obviously could not sing? Or so I was told. It has taken me a while, but gradually, because only God, the chipmunks, birds and I are listening, I have been able to allow these chants to flow through me. The chipmunks and birds don't cover their ears and take off and God doesn't seem to care whether I can carry a tune or not.

I remember at one of our workshops the moving experience of a man named Paul. He was about 50 and had spent some time a couple of years back in Medugorje. While he was there, he had a number of very powerful spiritual encounters that had prompted him, on his return, to write a book about his experiences there. The day of our workshop, he returned from an hour-long meditative walk through fields, woods and down along the water and shared his story with us. He told about his time in Medugorje and then told us that since he had been back from there, he was unable to pray. "Today on my walk I prayed," Paul told us with tears in his eyes. "For the first time since Medugorje, I feel hopeful that my relationship with God can be rekindled." We all sat silently for several moments after Paul spoke. How honored we felt to be present for this moment of homecoming.

✦

"I come to my solitary woodland walk as the homesick go home," Thoreau wrote.[44] Later in the same journal entry, he alludes to how his precious daily time in nature helped him to connect to God. "It is as if I always met in those places some grand, serene, immortal, infinitely encouraging, though invisible, companion, and walked with him." Thoreau, Emerson and the other New England Transcendentalists, were extolling time spent in nature as a pathway of transcendence from our ordinary perceptions and toward greater connectedness to the Creator. Most of the great spiritual teachers throughout history counsel us to spend time in nature and to let her teach us. Lao Tsu, the great Taoist teacher, advised his followers to listen to "the voice of the woods."[45] Jesus and Buddha were always wandering the countryside, using metaphors and stories from nature as teaching tools to awaken us to the great truths. Poets who, like these teachers, have an alternative perception and vision, use their poetry to open us to nature wisdom as a way to God and seeing the universe with different eyes. Blake's often repeated lines are familiar to most of us:

> To see the World in a Grain of Sand
> And Heaven in a Wild Flower
> Hold Infinity in the palm of your hand
> And Eternity in an hour.[46]

What Blake and others are saying is that the spiritual world lies hidden within each of us and beckons to us from

the physical world. Or as Robert Bly says, "Nature is one of the languages that God speaks."[47] Not only does She speak to us through the language of sages and prophets, but through the language of nature God helps us to "remember" and invites us to return home.

⁂

As I have pondered the fullness and complexity of my experience that day in the woods, I have come to understand aspects other than my spiritual longing to "go home." There is, for one, the physical aspect of home. Before my divorce, I had been living for 18 years in a place that was very much home to me. As one who identifies myself as a "walking around tree," I had sunk my roots deeply into the earth around that home. When I left there, I felt tremendously uprooted. I no longer had a home. Each day at the end of my work, I returned to a place, but it was not a home. And while I do have a home among people, with friends, my children and my mate, I have yet to find a physical place in which to sink my roots again.

This need for a place to call home is inherent in each of us and yet we express it differently. Jeanne's need for rootedness to a place is not as great as mine. Yes, she desires a place that is home, but seems to be more free to pick up and move on, setting down roots and nesting in the next place as long as it is a place she has chosen to be for a period of time. Some of us want the rootedness of being in one place for a long time. Others prefer the adventure of moving from one home to another. For myself, I long for the time when I can be rooted again. In the meantime, the woods is home for me. I ache with envy each time I read Thoreau or Muir and think how fortunate they were to spend endless hours just walking and being in the woods. Early each morning I walk down the road to the woods nearby and do my morning meditation in a cathedral-like grove of pines. People marvel that I am able to do this no matter what the weather or time of year. Little do they know that for me it is easy to get up and go into my beloved woods. It is the return trek that is difficult. Many mornings I think, "Someday I won't come back." I hope, one day, to have my home in the woods and then I will again sink my roots in deep with my Brother Trees.

My feeling of at-homeness in the woods grows with each passing day. How precious are those days when I take a few hours off from the madness and rush to the woods with great expectancy. Again Thoreau's words resonate deeply with me, "Ah, dear nature, the mere remembrance, after a short forgetfulness, of the pine woods! I come to it as a hungry man to a crust of bread."[48] While the woods is my home, other people feel at home in meadows, at beaches, rocky oceans, in mountains, caves, deserts, gardens, at lakes and so on. When I talk about this idea of a home in nature, people very quickly tell me where they feel most at home. Or, after a short guided visualization, they easily discover where their place in nature is. What is going on? The notion of a physical home in nature is central to our being. Once upon a time we were intimately connected to nature, reliant upon her as a partner in our daily life and deeply cognizant of her ways. Gradually, with the frequent mobility and "advances" of the industrial and technological ages, we moved farther and farther away from nature and a sense of connection to place. Yet, some part of us remembers in the very core of our being what it was like to be so connected and we feel the ache of this exile. The more time we spend in our places in nature, the more we reconnect to our "home."

While I am always at home in the woods, Jeanne's experience of at-homeness in nature is more fluid, fluctuating with her moods. She has to listen closely to her intuition. In a dark mood, she may one day want to walk along the edge of a turbulent ocean. Another day, into a forest as dark as her mood. If she is feeling expansive, she may want to feel the freedom of an open field. Another time, she may want to run along an endless expanse of sandy beach. It is a mystery why certain places feel more at home to each of us at certain times, but the feeling is undeniable. And it grows with more contact. A relationship develops. We feel a welcoming. The more we return to a familiar spot, the more welcome we feel. Our initial anxiety about being an outsider in an unfamiliar place gradually is transformed to a sense of deeper connection, a sense of at-homeness.

Our relationship with the other creatures can also be transformed. Our feelings of being separate from them is apparent in the comments we make: "Isn't that an interesting tree" or, "That's a beautiful bird. I wonder what it is." These remarks reflect the duality between observer and observed. We objectify the other creature. Over time, by returning repeatedly to the same spot, we develop a sense of kinship, partnership, friendship with the creatures that live there. This is reflected in our desire to touch the trees, climb over the

216

rocks, sleep in the meadow grass, be in the water. We have a sense of belonging, of being a part of the whole, of sharing the same home.

A while ago, while sitting under a tree doing my morning meditation, a fox trotted up within 20 feet of me. Bird in mouth, he had obviously just returned from the hunt. Startled, he backed up, dropped his catch and started barking. As I sat quietly, he walked away and then returned from another angle, barking again. This continued until I eventually left the woods. A few weeks later, again sitting in meditation, I sensed his presence nearby, looked up and saw a fox watching me from a distance. I decided to try to communicate. "Brother Fox," I said, "I mean you no harm. There's plenty of room in the forest for both you and me. We can share this space. You can trust that I will not harm you." Whether he "heard" me or not, I have no way of knowing, but since that day, whenever we encounter each other, the fox just pauses for a moment, looks at me and moves on. No more barking. Perhaps one day he'll walk up to me so that we can become closer friends. For now, we have an amicable relationship.

The idea of home is archetypal. It is a felt image that emerges from the collective unconscious so that, regardless of where we live or what culture we are raised in, we desire to have a physical place. It has to do also with a state of being. So the additional aspect of my experience in the woods that day, of wanting to go home, is the psychological aspect. The pain and guilt of my divorce had left me with a shattered sense of Self. Who was this man? I no longer knew. Not only had I lost my physical home, but I had lost my at-homeness with myself. Until that point, I had not realized the depths of the vestiges of a false Self, how much I was still molding myself to the expectations of others. With the divorce, that came crashing down and I was forced to create myself anew, to mold myself as if from an unworked mound of clay into a truer Self, to no one's expectations but my own. In large part, through my home in nature, I am recreating an at-homeness with my Self, a more complex, more fully alive, more spontaneous and delightfully unpredictable Self. Through her teachings and modeling to be who I really am, not to judge my self and because I cannot easily project my inner "stuff" onto nature, I feel a greater sense of wholeness and connection to my deeper Self. Of course, I do not always feel at home. In fact, feelings of at-homeness are transient. My desire is to have that feeling permanently, but the truth is that we are at home for a while and then we go away from home. We are homeless, searching for a new sense of Self, re-examining our relationships with others, with God, looking for a place in this world where we belong. Each period of homelessness requires psychological and/or spiritual work. We re-examine values, work, relationships; look for new meaning in our lives; search for deeper purpose. When our inner work is done, we have again come home. Each time we return with a greater and more permanent sense of at-homeness.

In our darkest times, we are not at home in any aspect of our lives. We do not know ourselves, relationships are lacking, we feel no sense of belonging, we are disconnected from God. In our most joyous times, we feel at home in all areas. Relationships, work and life in general flow and make sense. Or maybe they don't make sense, but then neither does it matter. We are living fully in our Self. Usually, we feel at home in some areas of life and not others. Do we ever reach a point where we always feel at home with Self, God and our place in this world? We think not. But the stretches of time when we are at home grow longer and the times away become fewer and farther between. Nature acts as a matrix, a womb, creating the place and space in which to come back to ourselves. Even when I am far away, there is great comfort in knowing the steadfastness of the woods. I return again and again to the place I feel most welcome, when it seems the world does not welcome me, or God has forgotten about my existence, or I am not welcoming with myself. In nature, I can know myself once again, as all the great religions teach that we must. Know thyself. In the midst of nature's ever-present diversity, I can come to accept my own complexity, the totality and uniqueness of who I am. How often we try to be other than who we really are! And, with such disastrous and painful consequences. In the refuge of my nature place, I can begin to remember who I am, put the pieces of my Self back together again. I can remember my relationship with God. And I can find, once again, my home, a place of belonging within the whole of this Creation.

222

# NOTES

## Awakenings

1 John Fowles, *The Tree*. The Nature Company, Berkeley, 1994, p. 41.

2 Ralph Waldo Emerson, *Nature and Other Writings*. Shambhala, Boston, 1994, p. 6.

3 Emerson, *Nature and Other Writings*. p. 7.

## Presence

4 Kahlil Gibran, *The Prophet*. Alfred A. Knopf, New York, 1923, p. 58.

5 author unknown, edited by William Johnston, *The Cloud of Unknowing*. Image, New York, 1973.

6 Henry David Thoreau, *Walking*. The Nature Company, Berkeley, 1993, p. 31.

7 Richard Powers as quoted in *Songs of the Earth*. Running Press, Philadelphia, 1995, p. 18.

8 Thoreau, *Walking*. p. 12

9 Emerson, *Nature and Other Writings*. p. 7.

## Solitude

10 M. Esther Harding, *Women's Mysteries; Ancient and Modern*. G.P. Putnam's Sons, New York, 1971, p. 125.

11 David A. Cooper, *Silence, Simplicity and Solitude*. Bell Tower, New York, 1992, p. 13.

## Caretakers

12 Black Elk as quoted in *This Sacred Earth: Religion, Nature, Environment.* Routeledge, New York, 1996, p. 140.

13 St. Francis as quoted in *This Sacred Earth: Religion, Nature, Environment.* p. 122.

## Intimacy

14 Thomas Moore, *Soul Mates: Honoring the Mysteries of Love and Relationship.* Harper Collins, New York, 1994, p. 23.

15 Maya Angelou as quoted in *Songs of the Earth.* p. 22.

16 Diane Ackerman, *A Natural History of the Senses.* Vintage, New York, 1990, p. 13.

17 Jane Goodall as quoted in the *Ecopsychology Newsletter,* 1996

18 Anita Barrows as quoted in the *Ecopsychology Newsletter,* 1996

19 John Muir as quoted in *Songs of the Earth.* p. 48.

## Simplicity

20 Thich Nhat Hanh, *Being Peace.* Parallax Press, Berkeley, 1987.

21 Thich Nhat Hanh, *The Miracle of Mindfulness: A Manual on Meditation.* Beacon Press, Boston, 1975, p. 27.

22 Virginia Woolf, *A Room of One's Own.* Hardcourt Brace & Company, London, 1929.

## Self-Forgiveness

23 Discussion of unhealthy guilt comes from Joan Borysenko, *Guilt is the Teacher, Love is the Lesson*. Warner, New York, 1990, p. 9.

24 as quoted in *The Gnostic Gospels* by Elaine Pagels; Vintage Books, New York 1989, p.126.

25 Joan Borysenko, *Guilt is the Teacher, Love is the Lesson*. Warner, New York, 1990, p. 181.

26 Larry Dossey, *Healing Words: The Power of Prayer and the Practice of Medicine*. Harper Collins, San Francisco, 1993, p. 24.

## Gardens

27 Marilyn Barrett as quoted in "Secrets of the Garden", Article by Daphne White in *Common Boundary*. March/April 1994, p. 43

28 Story about Topler Delaney in "Gardens That Heal', by Diana Ketchum in *Self*. May 1996, p. 183.

## Path

29 Buddha as quoted in *This Sacred Earth: Religion, Nature, Environment*. p. 148.

30 Abraham Ibu Ezra as quoted in *This Sacred Earth: Religion, Nature, Environment*. p. 93.

31 Baal Shem Tov as quoted in *This Sacred Earth: Religion, Nature, Environment*. p. 94.

32 Emerson, *Nature and Other Writings*. p. 3.

33 Black Elk as quoted in *This Sacred Earth: Religion, Nature, Environment*. p. 140.

34 O Great Spirit, chant from tape, Spring Hill Music, 1989.

35 Quote from Book of Job as it appears in *This Sacred Earth: Religion, Nature, Environment.* p. 89.

36 St. Francis as quoted in *This Sacred Earth: Religion, Nature, Environment.* p. 122.

37 Ram Dass from tape of *Conscious Aging: On the Nature of Change and Facing Death.* Recorded by Sounds True at Conscious Aging Conference in New York sponsored by the Omega Institute.

38 James Carney is a friend of Bill's who gave permission to include his poem.

## Darkness

39 Robert Bly as quoted in "A Gathering of Men", transcript of a Public Affairs Television interview of Robert Bly by Bill Moyers, 1990.

40 Robert Assagioli, *Psychosynthesis.* Penguin, New York, 1976.

41 Donna Reed, documentary entitled *The Burning Times.* Distributed by Direct Cinema Limited, Santa Monica, California.

42 Wendell Berry as quoted in *The Earth Speaks.* Edited by Steve Van Matre and Bill Weiler, The Institute for Earth Education, Greenville, 1983, p. 158.

## Home

43 William Shakespeare as quoted in *Songs of the Earth.* p. 45.

44 Henry David Thoreau from a journal entry of Thoreau's as quoted in Robert Bly's *The Winged Life: The Poetic*

*Voice of Henry David Thoreau.* Sierra Club Books, San Francisco, 1986, p. 11.

45 Lao Tsu as quoted in *This Sacred Earth: Religion, Nature, Environment.* p. 67.

46 William Blake, from his poem "Auguries of Innocence" as quoted in *The Winged Life: The Poetic Voice of Henry David Thoreau.* p. 109.

47 Bly, *The Winged Life: The Poetic Voice of Henry David Thoreau.* p. 78.

48 Henry David Thoreau from a journal entry of Thoreau's as quoted in Bly's *The Winged Life: The Poetic Voice of Henry David Thoreau.* p. 108.

Photo by Sarah Ryan

## ABOUT THE AUTHORS

Jeanne Lightfoot and Bill Ryan both recently began to put down roots in the woods in Ashfield, MA.

Bill is a psychologist and co-author of *Love Blocks; Breaking The Patterns That Undermine Relationships*. In his spare time he can be found sauntering along the trails of Bear Swamp Reservation, stopping at the ledge for a cup of tea, and always keeping an eye out for a porcupine, a bear, or "something".

Jeanne is a poet, essayist and psychotherapist. She likes to build stone walls, wander along the brook, gather sticks and "stuff" and work in their garden.

Bill and Jeanne have private practices in Shelburne Falls, MA and Huntington, NY.

## ABOUT THE ARTIST

"The inspiration for my drawings," Karin Ralph says, "came from a series of rambles with Jeanne and Bill as well as days abroad with my dog. I love being out walking, and to go adventuring with two friends who share kinship with our beautiful earth, makes it even better. Visiting old haunts and new, reseeing places with other eyes led to the illustrations in this book. They became meditations. I used the tools of a sumie artist (even though I am not one): stone, ink, stick and brush. Stone, pigment, water: the elements transmuted into a magical process, a quiet contemplation."